SCHOLASTIC

ACTIVE™ English 7

Coursebook

Name: ______________________________

Class: ______________________________

Text Credits

The Three Precious Packets from *Tales of China* retold by Cyril Birch (OUP, 2000), copyright © Cyril Birch 1961, reprinted by permission of Oxford University Press; *Roll of Thunder, Hear My Cry* by Mildred D. Taylor, first published by Dial Press, 1976; *The Trial* from *The Kick Off* by Dan Freedman (Scholastic UK: 2007); *The Spirit of Cricket* by Sunil Gavaskar from *The Scholastic Book of Historic Speeches* edited by Arunava Sinha (Scholastic India: 2006); Sampurna Chattarji for *Elevators and Escalators* from *The Fried Frog and Other Funny Freaky Foodie Feisty Poems* (Scholastic India: 2009); *Skelling* by David Almond, first published in the UK by Hodder Children's, an imprint of Hachette Children's Books, 338 Euston Road, London NW1 3BH; Scholastic UK for *The World in Your Room* from *Fantastic Future* (Scholastic UK: 2004).

Photo credits

Wikimedia
P9 © J.M.Garg; P10 © Kamalnv; P17 © Project Gutenberg; P19 © Mirza Rahim; P41 © Gnissah; P70 © Petr Kadlec, Nuno Tavares; P70 © Björn Láczay; P74 © Roberto Ferrari; P77 © BollywoodHungama.com; P 86 © A. Jake; P98 © Open English Web; P111 © Wilfred Pau; P134 © Darrenm540 at English Wikipedia; P135 © Beau Giles; P139 © Janto Dreijer; P148 © Nicholas Wang; P149 © Gamesingear; P152 © Derrick Mealiffe.

First edition 2012
Reprinted 2012, 2014 (thrice), 2015 (twice), 2016 (thrice), 2017 (thrice), 2018, 2020 (twice), 2021, 2022, 2023

ISBN-978-81-8477-734-5

Preface

The creators of ACTIVE **English** believe that literacy acquisition is dependent on the integrated teaching of reading, writing, listening and speaking skills, and the engagement of students. This integrated approach to learning and literacy development is advocated through a systematic and consistent instructional design and scope and sequence.

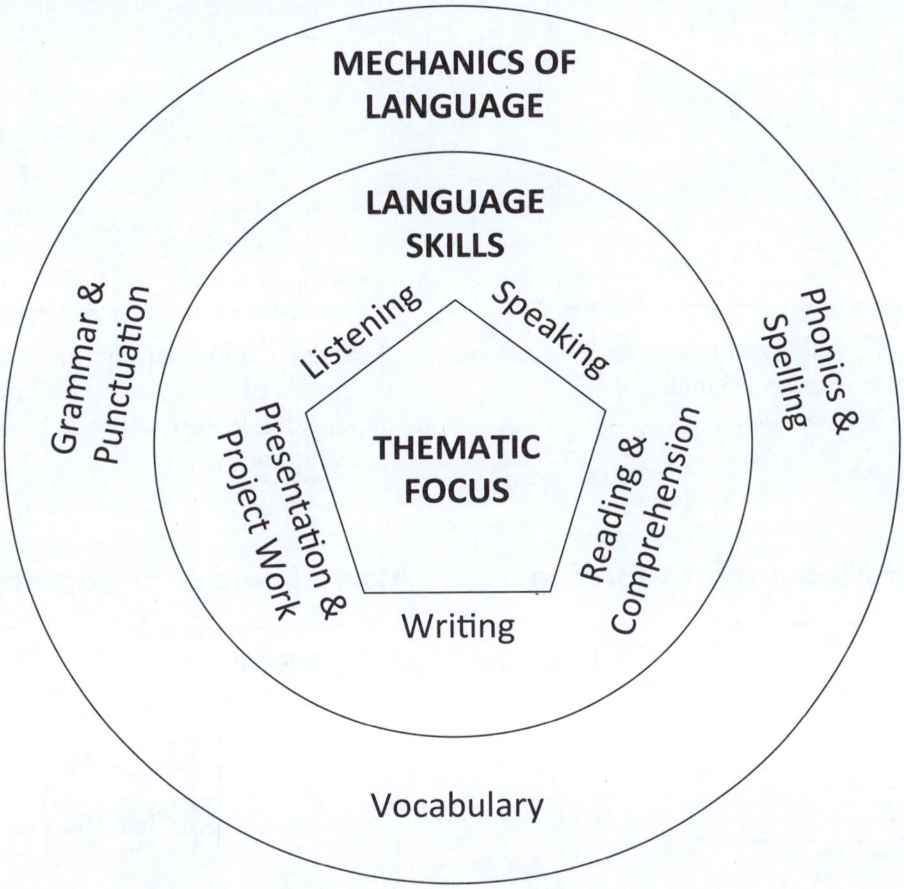

Each unit of the Coursebook has a thematic focus through which different language skills are meaningfully taught. Equal emphasis is given to each skill, enabling students to connect, transfer and build upon different skills.

Clear explanations and numerous examples give students a strong understanding of the mechanics of language and lay a strong foundation for good English.

As students progress through the levels, language skills are systematically taught at increasing levels of difficulty, allowing them to build upon small successes and reinforce the mechanics of language.

 ISBN-978-81-8477-734-5

Authentic and Varied Text Types

3 The Schoolboy

Read the following poem by William Blake, a famous English poet and artist. Blake belonged to a middle-class family and never went to school. He was known for his radical views on religion, society and other matters. This poem is from his *Songs of Innocence and of Experience.*

1 I love to rise in a summer morn,
When the birds sing on every tree;
The distant huntsman winds his horn,
And the skylark sings with me:
O what sweet company!

In what mood does the poem begin?

2 But to go to school in a summer morn, –
O it drives all joy away!
Under a cruel eye outworn,
The little ones spend the day
In sighing and dismay.

How does the mood shift in the second verse?

3 And then at times I drooping sit,
And spend many an anxious hour;
Nor in my book can I take delight,
Nor sit in learning's bower,
Worn through with the dreary shower.

Unit 3: The Schoolboy 37

Authentic texts in a variety of text types engage students and prepare them for language in the real world.

Effective Instructional Design

Grammar

Remember that **powerful verbs** can bring a piece of writing to life. They tell us not only about what is happening, but also about how the character feels.

Other than revealing how the character feels, a verb can also add to the image of the setting. For example, if it is a warm summer day and someone is **ambling** rather than **walking**, it encourages us to sense the warmth as well as visualise the character.

A. Find the following verbs in the excerpt and make short notes in the table about how you think the character feels.

Verb	How the character feels
lagged (paragraph 2)	
threatened (paragraph 3)	
glanced (paragraph 5)	
tugged (paragraph 6)	
dragged (paragraph 6)	
imprisoned (paragraph 6)	

B. In the following exercise, write two sentences for each of the situations, choosing verbs that not only reveal how the character feels, but also add something to the setting.

58 Theme 2: At School

A 'Show-Explain-Apply' methodology meets the needs of first generation English learners, making the lessons more achievable and boosting motivation.

Relevant and Meaningful Learning

Vocabulary

Can you remember what alliteration is? **Alliteration** is the repeated use of a particular letter or sound at the beginning of a number of words in a sentence.

Look at these examples:

silently **s**lipping away — *The "s" creates a soft or hissing sound.*

Escalators and Elevators — *The repetition of "e" (through the poem) re-inforces the sound.*

You can use sounds in all kinds of ways in poetry. Some of the well-known tongue twisters have alliterations in plenty. For example:

Betty **b**ought **b**utter **b**ut the **b**utter was **b**itter, so **B**etty **b**ought **b**etter **b**utter to make the **b**itter **b**utter **b**etter.

Wayne **w**ent to **W**ales to **w**atch **w**alruses.

When vowel sounds are repeated, we call this **assonance**:

p**ee**ling p**ea**ches

Did you notice that "peeling peaches" also includes alliteration? Another example of assonance is from one of the advertising slogans from 1950s about vacuum cleaners:

It b**ea**ts... as it sw**ee**ps... as it cl**ea**ns!

A. Based on your reading of the poem, answer the following questions.

1. Find examples of alliteration and assonance in the first two verses of the poem *Elevators and Escalators.*
2. Discuss with a partner what effect these sounds create in the poem.
3. Are you familiar with the ensuing tongue twisters? They are full of alliteration and assonance as well as repetition of other sounds. Can you identify the alliterations and assonances?

Unit 7: Elevators and Escalators 91

All language skills are meaningfully taught in the context of a theme, connecting the learning to real life and increasing learning enjoyment.

Active Learner Engagement

Activity

A storyboard is a series of illustrations created in sequence and is used to show the storyline or action of a film.

Create your own storyboard of frames for a simple animation.

1. Think of your own idea or choose from the following:
   - Dog wagging its tail
   - Hippopotamus yawning
   - Diver diving into a pool
   - Dancer leaping and landing
   - Bird flying
   - Blooming rose
   - A school kid
   - Fisherman and his fishing line

108 Theme 4: Our views

Activities throughout the units encourage students to actively participate and learn, improving retention and increasing the interaction between teacher and students.

 ISBN-978-81-8477-734-5

Ongoing and Accurate Assessment

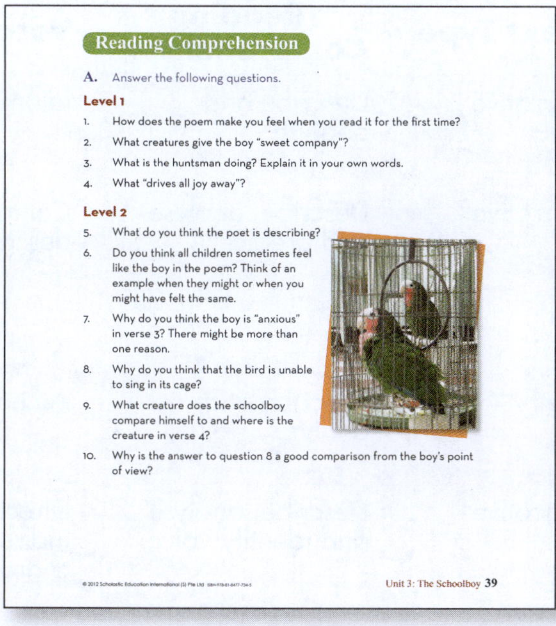

Reading Comprehension

A. Answer the following questions.

Level 1

1. How does the poem make you feel when you read it for the first time?
2. What creatures give the boy "sweet company"?
3. What is the huntsman doing? Explain it in your own words.
4. What "drives all joy away"?

Level 2

5. What do you think the poet is describing?
6. Do you think all children sometimes feel like the boy in the poem? Think of an example when they might or when you might have felt the same.
7. Why do you think the boy is "anxious" in verse 3? There might be more than one reason.
8. Why do you think that the bird is unable to sing in its cage?
9. What creature does the schoolboy compare himself to and where is the creature in verse 4?
10. Why is the answer to question 8 a good comparison from the boy's point of view?

Unit 3: The Schoolboy 39

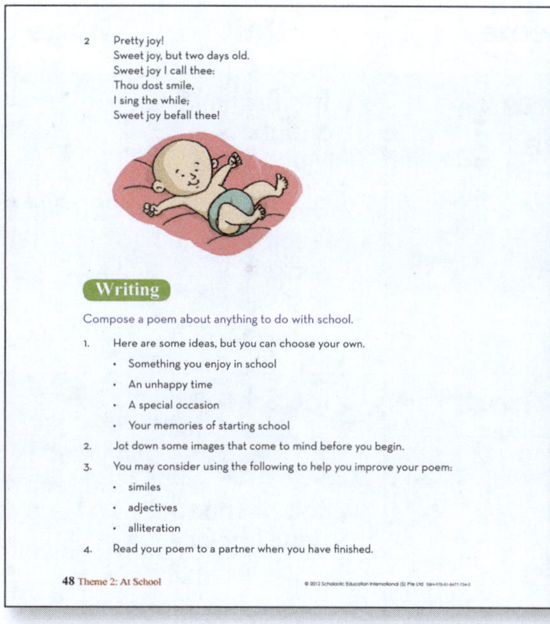

2 Pretty joy!
Sweet joy, but two days old.
Sweet joy I call thee:
Thou dost smile,
I sing the while;
Sweet joy befall thee!

Writing

Compose a poem about anything to do with school.

1. Here are some ideas, but you can choose your own.
   - Something you enjoy in school
   - An unhappy time
   - A special occasion
   - Your memories of starting school
2. Jot down some images that come to mind before you begin.
3. You may consider using the following to help you improve your poem:
   - similes
   - adjectives
   - alliteration
4. Read your poem to a partner when you have finished.

48 Theme 2: At School

Ongoing assessment throughout and end-of-lesson evaluation allow accurate assessment of students' understanding.

Diversity of Contexts

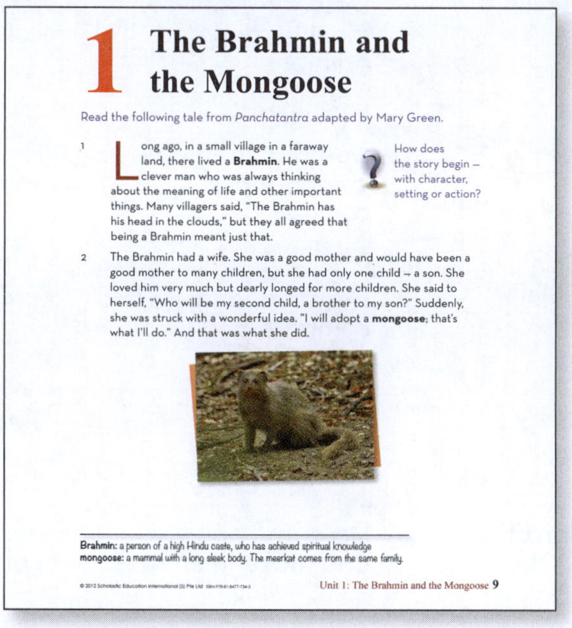

1 The Brahmin and the Mongoose

Read the following tale from *Panchatantra* adapted by Mary Green.

1 Long ago, in a small village in a faraway land, there lived a **Brahmin**. He was a clever man who was always thinking about the meaning of life and other important things. Many villagers said, "The Brahmin has his head in the clouds," but they all agreed that being a Brahmin meant just that.

How does the story begin – with character, setting or action?

2 The Brahmin had a wife. She was a good mother and would have been a good mother to many children, but she had only one child – a son. She loved him very much but dearly longed for more children. She said to herself, "Who will be my second child, a brother to my son?" Suddenly, she was struck with a wonderful idea. "I will adopt a **mongoose**; that's what I'll do." And that was what she did.

Brahmin: a person of a high Hindu caste, who has achieved spiritual knowledge
mongoose: a mammal with a long sleek body. The meerkat comes from the same family

Unit 1: The Brahmin and the Mongoose 9

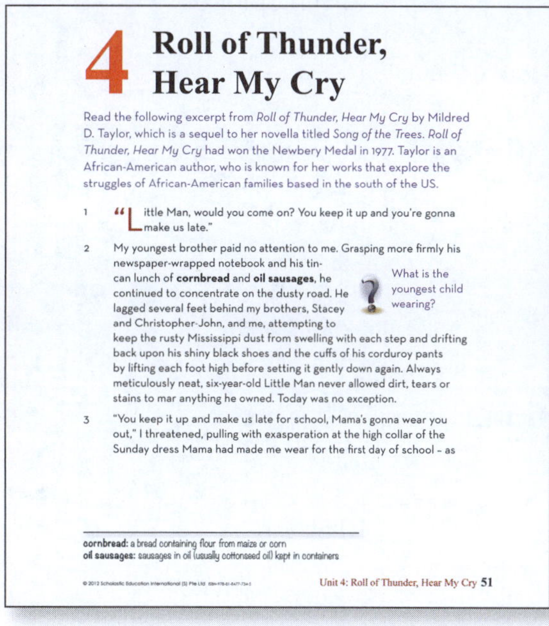

4 Roll of Thunder, Hear My Cry

Read the following excerpt from *Roll of Thunder, Hear My Cry* by Mildred D. Taylor, which is a sequel to her novella titled *Song of the Trees*. *Roll of Thunder, Hear My Cry* had won the Newbery Medal in 1977. Taylor is an African-American author, who is known for her works that explore the struggles of African-American families based in the south of the US.

1 "Little Man, would you come on? You keep it up and you're gonna make us late."

2 My youngest brother paid no attention to me. Grasping more firmly his newspaper-wrapped notebook and his tin-can lunch of **cornbread** and **oil sausages**, he continued to concentrate on the dusty road. He lagged several feet behind my brothers, Stacey and Christopher-John, and me, attempting to keep the rusty Mississippi dust from swelling with each step and drifting back upon his shiny black shoes and the cuffs of his corduroy pants by lifting each foot high before setting it gently down again. Always meticulously neat, six-year-old Little Man never allowed dirt, tears or stains to mar anything he owned. Today was no exception.

What is the youngest child wearing?

3 "You keep it up and make us late for school, Mama's gonna wear you out," I threatened, pulling with exasperation at the high collar of the Sunday dress Mama had made me wear for the first day of school – as

cornbread: a bread containing flour from maize or corn
oil sausages: sausages in oil (usually cottonseed oil) kept in containers

Unit 4: Roll of Thunder, Hear My Cry 51

Familiar contexts provide relevance while international contexts broaden students' perspectives and prepare them to take the global stage.

We hope that all students will have fun in becoming active participants in their own learning and they will enjoy every success in the learning of English!

Table of Contents

 ISBN-978-81-8477-734-5

Grammar/ Punctuation	Listening	Speaking	Writing	Activity
Declarative and Interrogative sentences	Listen to text on Aesop	Present a fable by Aesop	Write a character study of the Brahmin	Research on Indian folk tales
Main and subordinate clauses	Listen to the opening of a folk tale and predict what happens	Present the predictions from the tale in 'Listening'	Write your own folk tale	Compare the two tales in Theme 1
Semicolon	Listen to text on opportunities for children	Present a poem by William Blake	Compose a poem	Create a leaflet about William Blake
Powerful verbs	Listen to different points of view on a topic	Present your views about homework	Write an expository text about celebrities	Continue the story *Roll of Thunder, Hear My Cry* from a different point of view
Adverbs of manner, time and place	Listen to text about a traditional game	Give a short talk on an Indian sportsperson	Write a sports' report or a review of a competition or contest	Write a plan explaining how to carry out a successful penalty kick
Zero article	Listen to text about Dilip Doshi	Present a talk on sports	Write why sport is important for young people, stating your opinions	Write a code of behaviour for a game or sport
Forming adjectives	Listen to text on elevators	Present your views on elevators and escalators	Create a shape poem about an escalator or an elevator	Write about the Paternoster elevator
Comparatives and superlatives	Listen to text about 3D movies	Compare and contrast two movies	Write a review of a current TV programme	Create a storyboard
Infinitives	Listen to a riddle and work out its meaning	Discuss about family life	Compose a poem about an imaginary relative	Create a code of conduct for discussions
Tenses in narratives	Listen to text about David Almond for details	Predict and present what will happen in *Skellig*	Create an interesting setting	Review the 'Writing' task
Conditional clauses	Listen to text about virtual friends	Design and talk about your own futuristic gadget	Create an advertisement	Research on how people lived before machines and gadgets were invented
Modal verbs	Listen to comments on video games	Present your views on video games	Write an account about video games	Create a leaflet

 ISBN-978-81-8477-734-5

Theme 1

Learning Values

Look at the picture above and answer the following questions.

1. What is the setting of the picture?
2. How can you tell that it depicts a folk or fairy tale?
3. How can you tell that it might involve magic or the supernatural?
4. Describe everything you see in the picture.
5. Can you guess the name of the story? Read the story if you are not familiar with it.

 ISBN-978-81-8477-734-5

1 The Brahmin and the Mongoose

Read the following tale from *Panchatantra* adapted by Mary Green.

1 Long ago, in a small village in a faraway land, there lived a **Brahmin**. He was a clever man who was always thinking about the meaning of life and other important things. Many villagers said, "The Brahmin has his head in the clouds," but they all agreed that being a Brahmin meant just that.

How does the story begin – with character, setting or action?

2 The Brahmin had a wife. She was a good mother and would have been a good mother to many children, but she had only one child – a son. She loved him very much but dearly longed for more children. She said to herself, "Who will be my second child, a brother to my son?" Suddenly, she was struck with a wonderful idea. "I will adopt a **mongoose**; that's what I'll do." And that was what she did.

Brahmin: a person of a high Hindu caste, who has achieved spiritual knowledge
mongoose: a mammal with a long sleek body. The meerkat comes from the same family.

 ISBN-978-81-8477-734-5

3 It was a fine specimen, and the Brahmin's wife looked after him just as she would her own child. She washed and fed him with great care, and the mongoose and the son became like brothers.

4 One day, the wife had to collect water from the well. It was a hot, dusty day and the sun was at its highest. She did not want to take either of her children with her. She told her husband, "We need fresh water. I must go to the well. Can you please look after our sons?" As usual, the Brahmin was lost in his thoughts. "Do you hear me?" she repeated.

5 The Brahmin nodded his head, but who knows whether he heard her or not. About ten minutes later, he wandered off and sat under a shady tree to think more deeply about an important matter that had been troubling him.

6 Unknown to anyone, a snake had been lying hidden in a corner of the room. He was hungry, very hungry, and his tongue flicked in and out. He sidled towards the baby – slowly at first then more quickly, for snakes can move fast when they want to. The baby was lying gurgling and laughing, quite unaware of how close he was to danger.

7 But the mongoose knew. All his natural instincts told him he must act. In a trice, he leapt on the snake just as it was about to climb onto the mat. He fought with the snake and killed it.

8 Rushing out of the house, the mongoose ran to the well to meet his mother. He would tell her what had happened and how brave he had been. But the moment his mother saw him, she caught her breath in horror. Seeing the blood trickling from his mouth, she feared the worst. "The mongoose has killed my baby! The mongoose has killed my baby!" These were the only words that ran through her head and she picked up a heavy stick and killed the mongoose with one blow. He lay at her feet, quiet and still.

How would you describe the actions of the wife?

 ISBN-978-81-8477-734-5

9 She hurried home as quickly as she could, forgetting her jar of water. And what did she find? On the rush mat lay her baby safe and sound, with not a mark on him. Beside him, lay the dead snake.

10 Realising what had happened, she began to wail unconsolably. Tears streamed down her face. When the Brahmin came back, she turned to him in anger and sadness.

11 "You did not do your duty. You failed your children and must know the pain of grief and loss, for nothing will bring back our son."

12 The Brahmin sat with his head in his hands. He then left the house to bring back the body of his dead mongoose child.

How was the Brahmin feeling at this point?

Reading Comprehension

A. Answer the following questions.

Level 1

1. Where and when is the story set?
2. Name all the characters in the story. Who do you think are the main characters?
3. What did the Brahmin spend his time doing?
4. Why did the mongoose come to live with the Brahmin and his wife?
5. When does the problem arise in the story?
6. What is the high point of the story?

Level 2

7. What regrets do you think the Brahmin's wife had at the beginning of the story?
8. Apart from the comments you made in the previous question, what kind of a person do you think was the Brahmin's wife?

 ISBN-978-81-8477-734-5

9. Describe the characteristics of the mongoose and the snake.
10. How can you tell that the story is a folk tale?

B. Read about folk and fairy tales. Work in a small group of three or four and discuss the following questions.

Level 3

Many folk and fairy tales and stories, such as fables, have a moral. This is the message or lesson that the story teaches us.

11. Who do you think was responsible for the mongoose's death? Was it one character or more than one?
12. What might have prevented the mongoose's death?
13. What did the characters learn at the end of the tale?
14. What do you think is the moral behind *The Brahmin and the Mongoose*?
15. Do you agree with the moral? Why or why not? Hold a group discussion and record your views in the given template.

Moral behind *The Brahmin and the Mongoose*:		
Group members	**Views**	**Reasons**

In conclusion, the group decided that...

 ISBN-978-81-8477-734-5

Vocabulary

An **idiom** is a fixed combination of words that has a particular meaning, which usually cannot be guessed from the meanings of the individual words themselves. For example:

It **rained cats and dogs** last night.

A. The following sentence is from *The Brahmin and the Mongoose.* What does the idiom mean?

Many villagers said, "The Brahmin has his **head in the clouds**," but they all agreed that being a Brahmin meant just that.

B. Match each idiom on the left to its meaning on the right.

Idiom	Meaning
barking up the wrong tree	take on more than you can manage
as right as rain	focusing in the wrong place when trying to find out something
under the weather	joking, not to be taken seriously
burn the midnight oil	feeling well and happy
by the skin of your teeth	feeling ill
bite off more than you can chew	work late into the night
tongue in cheek	a narrow escape

 ISBN-978-81-8477-734-5

C. Find a single word to replace the underlined idiom in each of the following sentences.

1. Fred won't get any of the money until his Dad <u>kicks the bucket</u>.
2. I think that you should <u>keep an eye on</u> the man in the grey jacket. He's been behaving rather suspiciously.
3. Paul says that he's feeling <u>under the weather</u> and won't be able to come this evening.
4. Job opportunities are rather <u>thin on the ground</u> at present.
5. That man's being a real <u>pain in the neck</u>. He just won't stop asking questions.

Grammar

A **declarative sentence** makes a statement. Most sentences are declarative sentences. It begins with a capital letter and ends with a full stop. For example:

> **The Brahmin had a wife.**

An **interrogative sentence** asks a question. For example:

> **Did the Brahmin have a wife?**

You can make your narrative or expressive writing more interesting by introducing questions from time to time. For example:

> She hurried home as quickly as she could, forgetting her jar of water. **And what did she find?** On the rush mat lay her baby safe and sound, with not a mark on him. Beside him lay the dead snake.

The use of the interrogative sentence in the above example changes the tone of the voice and pace. It addresses the reader directly and is a "rhetorical" question – one that does not expect a reply.

 ISBN-978-81-8477-734-5

A. Replace the sentences that have been underlined in the passage with interrogative sentences that are appropriate in the context.

Example:

"... she saw something move. She could not see what it was."
" ... she thought she saw something move. What was it?"

Maria was sitting in a comfortable chair reading a book. Suddenly, out of the corner of her eye, she thought she saw something move. She could not see what it was. She turned her attention back to her book. Once again she thought she caught a flicker of movement over by the window. She wondered what it could be. She got up from her chair and tiptoed across the room. She couldn't see anything. Maybe her eyes had deceived her. Or maybe it was hiding somewhere. Gingerly Maria drew back the bottom of the curtain. Her eyes hadn't deceived her. There was a tiny mouse with its head in the folds of the curtain keeping utterly still ... like a child that thinks that if it can't see you, you can't see it. She asked herself whether she should pick it up. She decided not to. She was not scared of the mouse, but she was not entirely happy about the idea of having one in her hand. And it might bite her. A thought crossed her mind: this might not be the only mouse in her house. There might be a whole family of them.

B. Change the following declarative sentences into interrogative sentences.

1. Michael's aunt worked in a department store in town.
2. Mary does not care who disapproves of her.
3. The price of petrol went up again last week.
4. There is something wrong with Lucy's car.
5. His brother plays for the local soccer club.

 ISBN-978-81-8477-734-5

C. Write a paragraph about the mongoose and his character and introduce a question so that your writing sounds more interesting.

Remember

- The word "declare" is another word for "say".
- The word "interrogate" means "to question".

Listening

Listen to the text about Aesop and answer the questions given below.

1. Write short notes in the boxes.

Aesop

Who was he?

____

____

____

Where did he live?

____

____

____

2. What connection does he have with India?
3. What three fables are mentioned? List them in the table below.
4. What is a maxim?

 ISBN-978-81-8477-734-5

5. What maxim is given in the listening text? Record it in the table below, next to the correct fable.

Fable	Maxim

Speaking

Present any Aesop's fable to your group.

1. Choose the fable from the "Listening" section above.
2. Do some research on the fable.
3. Make brief notes about it.
4. Tell the story to your group without using notes.

THE TORTOISE AND THE HARE

 ISBN-978-81-8477-734-5

Speaking Tips

- Speak clearly and naturally.
- Try not to hesitate.
- Keep your eye level above the group when you are speaking so that you are not looking at faces, which can be distracting.
- If you make a mistake, correct yourself and carry on. Don't stop.

Writing

Write a character study of the Brahmin. You can do this using the concept map below. Consider the following points.

1. His main character traits
2. His relationships and their nature
3. What others say about him
4. What he does / doesn't do
5. The consequence of his choices
6. What he learns by the end of the story

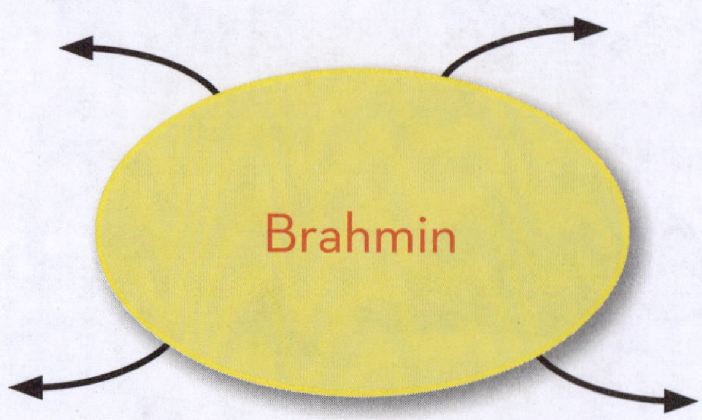

Remember that you can add new arrows or further branches from the existing arrows.

 ISBN-978-81-8477-734-5

Activity

Carry out a research on other Indian folk tales. They can be tales you know or that are new to you. Record the following data for each folk tale.

1. When does it date from
2. Main features (for example – magic, has animal characters, contains rhymes or jokes)
3. Main characters
4. Summary of the plot (include only a few sentences)
5. Whether or not it is a tale that appears in different cultures

(Note: If you use the Internet, work with your teacher's guidance.)

 ISBN-978-81-8477-734-5

2 The Three Precious Packets

Read this excerpt from *The Three Precious Packets* by Cyril Birch.

1 A poor student, whose name was Niu, was once travelling to the capital city for appearing in examinations. He decided to stay overnight in a village inn. It was the depth of winter, bitterly cold. Snow fell steadily from a leaden sky. Niu rejoiced in the warmth and comfort inside the inn. He sat toasting himself before a charcoal brazier and ordered hot soup and dumplings for his supper. While waiting for the food to arrive, he drove the chill from inside him with a bowl of hot rice-wine. Soon he felt a pleasant glow suffuse his whole body.

What word in the first sentence suggests a folk tale opening?

 ISBN-978-81-8477-734-5

2 The brief winter daylight was almost gone when a man knocked on the door and was admitted stumbling into the inn. He was poorer than Niu. His clothes were almost thin cotton rags, which was no proof against the keen weather. His cheeks were pinched, and he moved stiffly as though half-frozen. His lips were too numb to allow him to speak, but he cringed before Niu, obviously pleading to be allowed to share the warmth of the brazier.

3 Niu quickly made a place for him, and the man stretched his hands eagerly towards the glowing charcoal and began to thaw out gradually.

4 The landlord brought Niu's supper, the steam from which tickled the nostrils with a delicious smell. Then he turned to the ragged newcomer and asked what he could do for him.

5 "A bowl of tea, and a place on the floor for the night," said the man, and the landlord grunted and went off to fetch the tea.

6 Niu was filled with pity for this poor stranger. He pressed on him his own supper and, when the landlord came back, ordered more for himself. The stranger wolfed down the soup and dumplings in no time at all, and Niu ordered noodles to follow.

7 "I have no money to pay for them," said the man; but Niu insisted that he should accept them, and in no time five bowls of noodles had disappeared in the way the soup had. When they retired to rest, Niu tried to give up his own bed for the stranger to sleep on, but the man would not accept it. He lay down on the floor at the foot of the bed and slept immediately. As if to prove his satisfaction with the supper he had eaten, he snored like a bull all through the night.

8 As dawn was breaking, Niu was brought into wakefulness by someone gently shaking his shoulder. It was the stranger, who gazed at him with eyes full of affection. "Please come outside with me," he said. "I have something to say to you."

 ISBN-978-81-8477-734-5

9 Wonderingly Niu pulled on his boots and followed the man out of the door of the inn. In the cold grey light, the stranger turned to him and said, "I am not a human being, but an **envoy** from the underworld." Seeing Niu's look of fear, he added hastily, "Don't worry, I have not come for you. But I am very grateful for your kindness to me last night..."

How can we tell the stranger will be important in the story?

Reading Comprehension

A. Answer the following questions.

Level 1

1. Why was Niu travelling to the capital?
2. Where did he stop?
3. What time of the year was it and what was it like?
4. What did Niu drink to keep himself warm?
5. What two things did Niu do for the poor stranger?
6. Who was the stranger?

Level 2

7. How would you describe Niu? Use your own words.
8. How would you describe the stranger? Use your own words.
9. Can you explain why the stranger was presented like he was? What is the purpose of this?
10. What did the stranger think of Niu? How do you know?
11. What is the innkeeper like? How does he contrast with Niu?

---

envoy: messenger

 ISBN-978-81-8477-734-5

B. Read the following about predicting "what comes next" in a story or narrative and answer the questions given below.

Level 3

Making predictions or guessing what comes next can be tricky in a narrative. The writer will not give away too much because they want the reader to read on. But there are often clues that can help you make a judgement. In addition, you will be able to draw on your own experiences of stories you have read.

For example, think about the prior knowledge we all have about the fairy or folk tales. There are certain features specific to a folk tale. Some of these features are listed below.

- involvement of magic and luck
- offering us good advice
- rewards good actions and punishes bad ones
- focuses on surviving in a difficult world

12. Predict what comes next in the story, *The Three Precious Packets*. Some tips are given below for your help.

- Use clues from the story.
- Use your prior knowledge of traditional fairy or folk tales.
- Copy out the following writing frame and complete it to help you explain why you made the prediction, or use it as a guide and adapt it, as you need.

 ISBN-978-81-8477-734-5

When I read the excerpt from [name of story], I had some ideas about...

For example...

and also...

but I decided that...

My reasons for this choice are, firstly...

which suggests...

Secondly...

because...

Finally...

 ISBN-978-81-8477-734-5

Vocabulary

Contrasting descriptions are often used in narratives to make it more vivid and interesting.

How is the weather contrasted with the interior of the inn in the story, *The Three Precious Packets*? Read the following sentences.

Snow fell **steadily** (adverb) from a **leaden** (adjective) sky.

Soon he felt a **pleasant** (adjective) **glow** (noun) **suffuse** (powerful verb) his whole body.

Remember

- When a powerful verb such as "suffuse" is used, no adverb is needed.
- When a commonplace verb such as "fell" is used, an adverb such as "steadily" is suitable.

Adjectival phrases do the work of adjectives. They are often used in descriptions to add detail, as shown in the example.

The **snow-capped** mountains seemed to touch the sky.

A. Write a sentence to describe a chilly day contrasting it to the warmth of the sun.

 ISBN-978-81-8477-734-5

B. Write two contrasting paragraphs, choosing from the pairs below. Try to use some adjectival phrases.

1.

Winter

Summer

2.

Spring

Autumn

3.

Flood

Drought

4.

Storm

Stillness

 ISBN-978-81-8477-734-5

C. Fill in each blank in the passage with a suitable contrasting adjective from the box.

apprehensive	demonstrative	reserved	bashful
sociable	quiet		

Mike was going to stay with his Aunt Molly and Uncle Tom for a few days and he was feeling slightly ______________ about the visit. He liked his aunt and uncle and his three cousins very much, but they were a very ______________ family and Mike, like both his parents, was rather ______________. He was also rather ______________, particularly among people he did not know. His aunt was an extremely ______________ person and was always inviting people round for meals and giving parties. All this was a change from his own rather ______________ home. Still, he was looking forward to playing with his cousins Joe, Sam and Lucy. At least life at their house was never dull.

 ISBN-978-81-8477-734-5

Grammar

A **main clause** has a subject and a verb, and it makes sense on its own. A simple sentence is a main clause. For example:

subject (The stranger) — verb (opened)

The stranger opened the door.

Sometimes, a sentence can have two main clauses joined together by a conjunction such as "and", "but" or "or". Such sentences are **compound sentences**. You can call these main clauses co-ordinate clauses, as shown in the following example.

main clause (He loved mango chutney) — main clause (she loved lime pickle)

He loved mango chutney and **she loved lime pickle**.

A **subordinate clause** also has a subject and a verb, but it does not make sense on its own. It usually begins with words such as "because", "when", "which", "who". A subordinate clause can be joined to a main clause to form a complex sentence, as shown in the example below.

main clause (Niu ordered soup) — subordinate clause (because he was hungry)

Niu ordered soup because he was hungry.

Or we could say:

subordinate clause (Because he was hungry) — main clause (Niu ordered soup)

Because he was hungry, **Niu ordered soup**.

A. Underline the subject and circle the verb in each sentence.

1. Niu ordered soup.
2. The wind blew through the wood.
3. Flames flickered in the hearth.
4. The stranger thanked his new friend.

 ISBN-978-81-8477-734-5

B. Write three main clauses about the stranger and the landlord of the inn.

C. Create complex sentences with the following. You may need to add a subordinate clause or a main clause. You will also need to add the correct punctuation to your sentences.

1. which was dark and frightening
2. when the wind has passed
3. he gobbled up the food
4. the daylight had gone
5. how could he ignore the poor stranger

D. Underline the words in each of the following sentences that make up a subordinate clause.

1. The mayor, whose name is Hans Schmidt, will give a short speech.
2. The man told me that all the children had disappeared.
3. Shall we go out when Samira gets home?
4. We still don't know the reason why he left.
5. Because Mr Schmidt can't come tonight, his deputy will chair the meeting.
6. If the weather is fine, we may be able to go to the beach tomorrow.

 ISBN-978-81-8477-734-5

Listening

Listen to the opening from a folk tale and answer the questions.

1. Write short notes about the farmer.

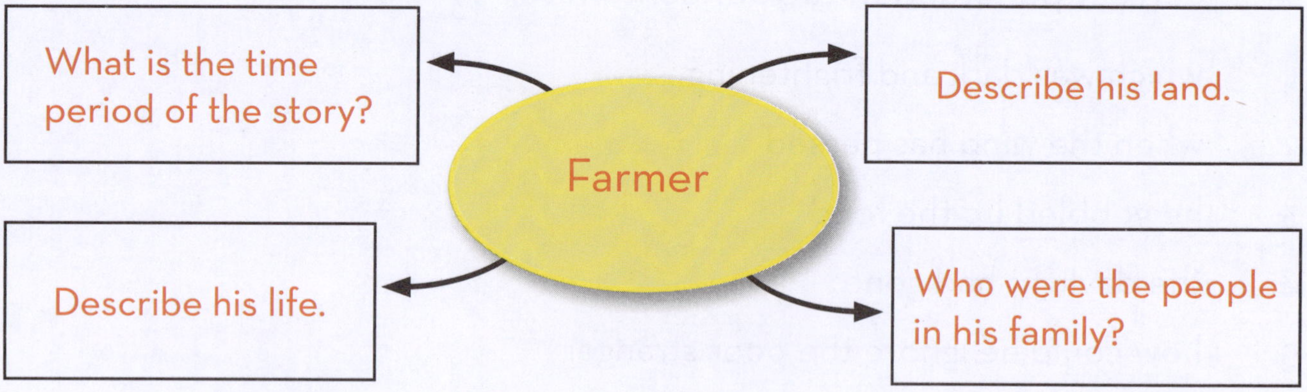

2. What did the farmer find? In what way might this be significant?
3. Predict what might happen and make notes.

 ISBN-978-81-8477-734-5

Speaking

Work in groups of three or four. Discuss what you think happened next in the folk tale which you heard in "Listening".

1. Each member of the group should present their own idea to the group. You can refer to the notes you made under "Listening" before beginning. However, once you begin, you should not refer to your notes.

2. Use the table below to help you record the ideas.

Group members	Ideas

3. When everyone has presented their ideas, decide as a group which idea is the most likely.

The group decided that the following idea is the most likely...

because...

 ISBN-978-81-8477-734-5

Writing

Write your own folk tale following the steps below.

1. Plan your folk tale using the following key headings:
   - Introduction – introduce the setting and characters
   - Complication – when a problem or obstacle occurs
   - Climax – the exciting highpoint of the tale
   - Resolution (or Conclusion) – when the problem is solved and things return to normal
2. Write at least 300 words of your story, including the Introduction and the Complication.
3. Give what you have written to a partner to read. They must work out what will happen and finish the story (write at least 300 words).
4. When your partner has finished, discuss how similar it was to your plan.

Remember

Don't let your partner see your plan!

 ISBN-978-81-8477-734-5

Activity

Compare The Brahmin and the Mongoose in Unit 1 with The Three Precious Packets.

1. Consider everything you have learned in Unit 1 as well as this unit and try to compare and contrast the two folk tales in as many ways as you can.
2. Copy out the table of similarities and differences below and complete it.

Comparing folk tales	
Similarities	**Differences**

3. Use your table to write an account comparing the two folk tales. You could organise your work in one of the two following ways.

 ISBN-978-81-8477-734-5

Method 1

- Write few paragraphs about one folk tale first.
- Then, follow it up by writing some paragraphs about the second folk tale, comparing and contrasting it to the first.

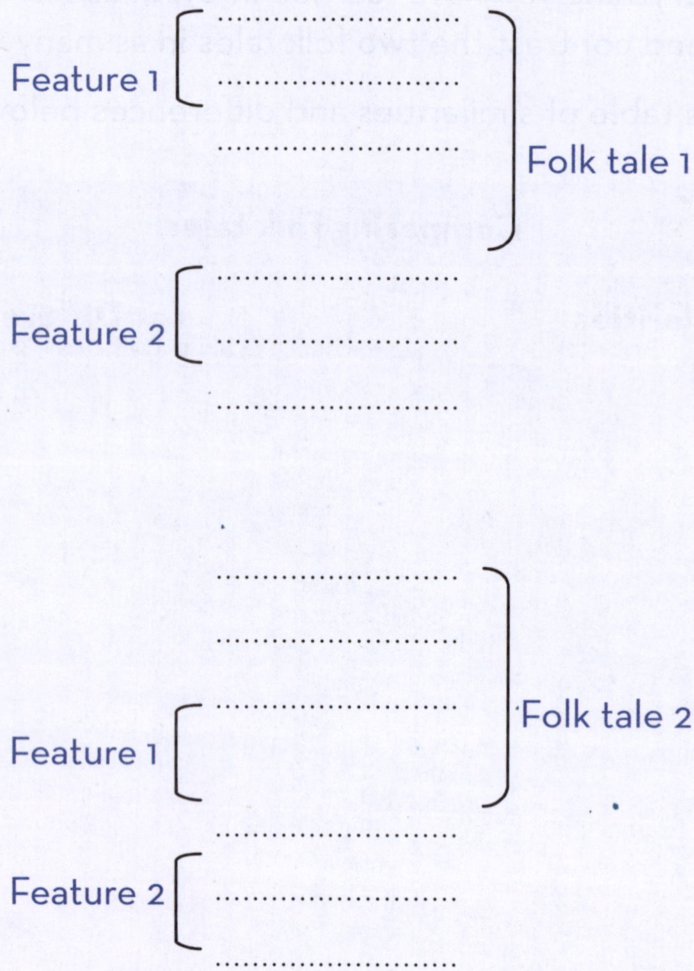

Method 2

This is a more structured method.

- Compare and contrast both folk tales as you write. So, you would begin with one feature first (such as, both are set in a distant past). This way you work through the features referring to both the folk tales.

 ISBN-978-81-8477-734-5

Feature 1 ....
....
....
.... Folk tale 1 and folk tale 2

....

....

Feature 2 ....
....
....
.... Folk tale 1 and folk tale 2

....

....

Whichever method you choose, you will need to use connectors of different kinds. For example, connectors of comparison and contrast:

Connectors of comparison	Connectors of contrast
In the same way...	On the other hand...
Equally...	Alternatively...

 ISBN-978-81-8477-734-5

Theme 2

At School

A. Look at the picture given above and answer the following questions.

1. What is the scene depicted in the picture? Describe the various features of the illustration.
2. What is the atmosphere in the scene like?
3. Look at the different people. How are they feeling?
4. How would you feel under similar circumstances?
5. In what way is this scene a common one across the world?

 ISBN-978-81-8477-734-5

3 The Schoolboy

Read the following poem by William Blake, a famous English poet and artist. Blake belonged to a middle-class family and never went to school. He was known for his radical views on religion, society and other matters. This poem is from his *Songs of Innocence and of Experience*.

1 I love to rise in a summer morn,
When the birds sing on every tree;
The distant huntsman winds his horn,
And the skylark sings with me:
O what sweet company!

In what mood does the poem begin?

2 But to go to school in a summer morn, –
O it drives all joy away!
Under a cruel eye outworn,
The little ones spend the day
In sighing and dismay.

How does the mood shift in the second verse?

3 And then at times I drooping sit,
And spend many an anxious hour;
Nor in my book can I take delight,
Nor sit in learning's bower,
Worn through with the dreary shower.

 ISBN-978-81-8477-734-5

4 How can the bird that is born for joy
Sit in a cage and sing?
How can a child, when fears annoy,
But droop his tender wing,
And forget his youthful spring!

5 O, father and mother if buds are nipped,
And blossoms blown away;
And if the tender plants are stripped
Of their joy in the springing day,
By sorrow and care's dismay,—

6 How shall the summer arise in joy,
Or the summer fruits appear?
Or how shall we gather what griefs destroy,
Or bless the mellowing year,
When the blasts of winter appear?

Who does the child in the poem speak to towards the end?

 ISBN-978-81-8477-734-5

Reading Comprehension

A. Answer the following questions.

Level 1

1. How does the poem make you feel when you read it for the first time?
2. What creatures give the boy "sweet company"?
3. What is the huntsman doing? Explain it in your own words.
4. What "drives all joy away"?

Level 2

5. What do you think the poet is describing?
6. Do you think all children sometimes feel like the boy in the poem? Think of an example when they might or when you might have felt the same.
7. Why do you think the boy is "anxious" in verse 3? There might be more than one reason.
8. Why do you think that the bird is unable to sing in its cage?
9. What creature does the schoolboy compare himself to and where is the creature in verse 4?
10. Why is the answer to question 8 a good comparison from the boy's point of view?

 ISBN-978-81-8477-734-5

B. Differentiate between simile and metaphor.

Level 3

Do you know the difference between a simile and a metaphor? Both make comparisons, but a simile uses "as" or "like" as shown in the following example.

The fireflies shone **like** tiny eyes, twinkling among the trees.

A metaphor replaces one thing with another:

Tiny eyes twinkled among the trees.

11. The poem, *The Schoolboy*, is full of metaphors. What do you think these could mean?
    - cruel eye (verse 2)
    - learning's bower (verse 3)
    - droop his tender wing (verse 4)
    - buds (verse 5)
    - tender plants (verse 5)

 ISBN-978-81-8477-734-5

12. A lion is commonly used as a metaphor for strength and power. What do you think these creatures could represent? Write down your ideas.

Creature	Idea
tortoiseshell cat	
parrot	
polar bear	
ant	
beaver	
prawn	
monkey	
hippopotamus	

 ISBN-978-81-8477-734-5

Vocabulary

Words that are **archaic** are no longer or rarely used. Since the poem was written a long time ago, it contains archaic words. Some of the words we use today will become archaic in turn.

A. Refer to the poem. Can you guess the meaning of these words?

1. morn
2. winds
3. outworn
4. bower

B. Do you know the meaning of the archaic words in bold below? Rewrite the sentences in modern English. Try to make your sentences sound natural.

1. "**Yonder** is the stream," **quoth** she.
2. **Whither dost thou go**?
3. Have you lost your **wits**?
4. **Thither** he comes.
5. **Call'st** thou me foolish?
6. Thou **know'st** not **whereof** thou **speak'st**.
7. I saw a **fair maiden** sitting on a stone.
8. Thither I will go. **Wilt** thou come with me?

 ISBN-978-81-8477-734-5

C. Fill in the blanks in the passage with appropriate words from the box.

lay waste	'twas	hence	hail
quoth	forth	trusty	steed

"____________, fair mistress!" The knight reined in his milk-white ____________ and dismounted. "Say who thou art and what villain hath chained thee to this rock."

"Begone and leave me to my fate, sir knight," ____________ the damsel. "I am the Princess Eleanor. ____________ my own father, King Cuthbert, who chained me to this rock, though many a tear he wept the while. I must be sacrificed to a dreadful dragon who else will ____________ all the kingdom. Quick, quick, sir knight, get thee ____________, the dragon cometh even now."

With a fearsome roar and a hideous clash of his scaly wings, the dragon alighted, spitting – ____________ fire and smoke. Nothing daunted, the knight leapt back into his saddle. He took his ____________ lance in his strong right hand, set spurs to his mount and charged.

 ISBN-978-81-8477-734-5

Grammar

Do you know when we use the **semicolon** (;)? In the past, it was used more often than we use it these days. There are examples of the semicolon in the poem, *The Schoolboy*, in verses 1, 3 and 5. Nowadays, poets would probably not include it.

We can use the semicolon, in place of a conjunction, to give additional information, particularly if we want to sound sharper or more precise. It is a slightly longer pause than a comma.

> Deepak was late for school every day**;** he hated seeing the towering school gates.

You could replace the semicolon with the conjunction "and".

> Deepak was late for school every day **and** he hated seeing the towering school gates.

Commas are frequently used to separate items in a list that follows a colon (:), especially if the items are relatively short.

> There are four things that life has taught me: not to tell lies, not to shirk my duties, not to stay up late, and be polite to girls.

Longer items in a list should be separated by semicolons.

> There are four things that life has taught me: not to tell lies even to escape severe punishment; not to shirk my duties even if it means missing my leisure time; not to stay up late if i have school the next day; and to be polite to girls, especially as they are the ones who help you with your homework.

 ISBN-978-81-8477-734-5

A. Pair each clause in **A** with the correct one in **B**. They should be joined by a semicolon. Also suggest what conjunction could be used instead.

A	B
Mina had to collect her little sister.	He could hardly lift it.
The computer crashed.	I enjoy the holidays more.
The school bag was so heavy.	All the children, except one, got into line.
The bell went.	Her little sister was late.
I enjoy school.	The screen went completely blank.

B. Insert semicolons into the following sentences, each of which ends with a list.

1. Mary opened her suitcase and took out the following items: a bright red two-piece swimming costume that she bought in the sales a very large towel to lie on beside the swimming pool or on the beach two bottles of suntan lotion and the latest novel by Matilda Smith.
2. There are a number of things we have to do before we go on holiday: take the car to the garage to have it checked inform the next-door neighbours that we shall be away for two weeks ask someone to feed the cat while we are away and make sure that all the doors and windows are securely locked.
3. The guest list included: Ravi Chatterjee, professor of political economy at the University of Bombay Julia Andante, the famous Italian scientist and inventor Maria T. Shoemaker, chairwoman and chief executive of the Alphastick Corporation of San Francisco and best-selling author and TV personality, Rudolph Chang.

 ISBN-978-81-8477-734-5

4. Let's just remind ourselves of what we've done already: we've assembled all the ingredients that we need to make the dish we've brought together the pots and pans that we need and checked that they are clean we have sliced the meat and chopped up all the vegetables ready to go in the pan we have turned on the oven to allow it to heat up. No we can start cooking!

C. Six semicolons are missing from the passage. Put them back where they ought to be.

Martha was feeling very tired her head was aching and her feet were sore. It had been a very long day in the shop. For most of the day, customers had arrived in ones and twos. Towards the end of the afternoon, however, business had suddenly picked up. A dozen customers had arrived at once all of them were impatient to be served. All the other counters were equally busy consequently, there was no one able to help Martha. She rushed to and fro between the shelves and the till. She had sold an awful lot of perfume and taken an awful lot of money she had expended an awful lot of energy too. Then there was the journey home on the crowded bus. It was hot, very hot everyone was complaining about the heat. But now she was home at last. Did she dare sit down before she prepared the evening meal? The risk was that she might fall asleep and not wake up until late at night. But she had to sit down she had no choice but to sit down. She sat down. Then it was midnight.

Listening

Listen to the account and answer the following questions.

1. What kind of children in the passage do not attend school?
2. What kind of jobs might the children do on the street?
3. What does "work... in the fields" mean?
4. Why don't the children attend school?

 ISBN-978-81-8477-734-5

5. What do you think the expression "They are old before their years" means?

Speaking

Read the following poem by William Blake to a group.

1. There are some archaic words included. Can you guess what they mean?
2. Try to learn the poem by heart.
3. Briefly introduce the poem before you begin.

Infant Joy

1 "I have no name;
I am but two days old."
What shall I call thee?
"I happy am,
Joy is my name."
Sweet joy befall thee!

 ISBN-978-81-8477-734-5

2 Pretty joy!
Sweet joy, but two days old.
Sweet joy I call thee:
Thou dost smile,
I sing the while;
Sweet joy befall thee!

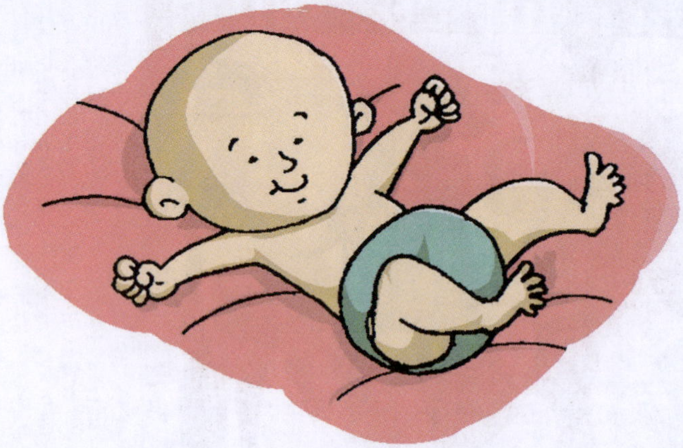

Writing

Compose a poem about anything to do with school.

1. Here are some ideas, but you can choose your own.
   - Something you enjoy in school
   - An unhappy time
   - A special occasion
   - Your memories of starting school
2. Jot down some images that come to mind before you begin.
3. You may consider using the following to help you improve your poem:
   - similes
   - adjectives
   - alliteration
4. Read your poem to a partner when you have finished.

 ISBN-978-81-8477-734-5

Remember

- Your poem does not have to rhyme.
- You could have repeating words or lines (such as "I remember").

Activity

William Blake was an important English poet who wrote many poems, some about children. He was also a painter and printer. One of his famous books is *The Songs of Innocence and of Experience*, from which *The Schoolboy* has been taken.

Do a research on William Blake and create a leaflet about him. Here are some points you may keep in mind while doing the research.

1. Find out the following about him.
   - When did he live?
   - Where did he live?
   - Whom did he marry?
   - What kind of school do you think he would have supported?

 ISBN-978-81-8477-734-5

2. What else can you find out about William Blake?

3. Create a leaflet about him.

- Write a brief note about what William Blake was like.
- Use the skills you have previously learned. For instance, create a timeline of important events in his life or a fact file.
- Include a poem of his that you like.
- Add your own illustrations.
- Present your leaflet in a way that you think would appeal to the reader.

 ISBN-978-81-8477-734-5

4 Roll of Thunder, Hear My Cry

Read the following excerpt from *Roll of Thunder, Hear My Cry* by Mildred D. Taylor, which is a sequel to her novella titled *Song of the Trees*. *Roll of Thunder, Hear My Cry* had won the Newbery Medal in 1977. Taylor is an African-American author, who is known for her works that explore the struggles of African-American families based in the south of the US.

1 "Little Man, would you come on? You keep it up and you're gonna make us late."

2 My youngest brother paid no attention to me. Grasping more firmly his newspaper-wrapped notebook and his tin-can lunch of **cornbread** and **oil sausages**, he continued to concentrate on the dusty road. He lagged several feet behind my brothers, Stacey and Christopher-John, and me, attempting to keep the rusty Mississippi dust from swelling with each step and drifting back upon his shiny black shoes and the cuffs of his corduroy pants by lifting each foot high before setting it gently down again. Always meticulously neat, six-year-old Little Man never allowed dirt, tears or stains to mar anything he owned. Today was no exception.

What is the youngest child wearing?

3 "You keep it up and make us late for school, Mama's gonna wear you out," I threatened, pulling with exasperation at the high collar of the Sunday dress Mama had made me wear for the first day of school – as

---

cornbread: a bread containing flour from maize or corn
oil sausages: sausages in oil (usually cottonseed oil) kept in containers

 ISBN-978-81-8477-734-5

if that event were something special. It seemed to me that showing up at school at all on a bright August-like October morning made for running the cool first trails and wading barefoot in the forest pond was concession enough; Sunday clothing was asking too much. Christopher-John and Stacey were not too pleased about the clothing or school either. Only Little Man, just beginning his school career, found the prospects of both intriguing.

4 "Y'all go ahead and get dirty if y'all wanna," he replied without even looking up from his studied steps. "Me, I'm gonna stay clean."

How does the youngest child react to being told off?

5 Christopher-John, walking between Stacey and me, glanced uneasily at both of us but did not interfere. A short round boy of seven, he took little interest in troublesome things, preferring to remain on good terms

 ISBN-978-81-8477-734-5

with everyone. Yet he was always sensitive to others and now, shifting the handle of his lunch can from his right hand to his right wrist and his smudged notebook from his left hand to his left armpit, he stuffed his free hands into his pockets and attempted to make his face as moody as Stacey's and as cranky as mine. But after a few moments, he seemed to forget that he was supposed to be grouchy and began whistling cheerfully. There was little that could make Christopher-John unhappy for very long, not even the thought of school.

6 I tugged again at my collar and dragged my feet in the dust, allowing it to sift back onto my socks and shoes like gritty red snow. I hated the dress. And the shoes. There was little I could do in a dress, and as for shoes, they imprisoned freedom-loving feet accustomed to the feel of the warm earth.

7 "Cassie, stop that," Stacey snapped as the dust billowed in swirling clouds around my feet. I looked up sharply, ready to protest. Christopher-John's whistling increased to a raucous, nervous shrill, and grudgingly I let the matter drop and trudged along in moody silence, my brothers growing as pensively quiet as I.

 ISBN-978-81-8477-734-5

Reading Comprehension

A. Answer the following questions.

Level 1

1. Where are the children going?
2. What kind of weather is described in the story?
3. What time of year is it?
4. What food are they carrying for lunch?
5. How many characters are there in the excerpt and who are they?
6. What other character is referred to but is not present in this excerpt?

Level 2

7. Can you guess where the story is set?
8. Why are the characters finding it difficult to make progress?
9. What impression does the excerpt leave on you?
10. Which character leaves the greatest impression on you and why?

B. Read the following note about "voice" or narrative voice and answer the questions given below.

Level 3

A story is told by a narrator, that is, a "voice" is telling us what is happening. We see things from their point of view. Sometimes a character, usually the main character, tells the story.

11. In what person is the excerpt written, first or third?
12. Consider your answer to question 11 and say from whose point of view is the story written – in other words, who is the narrator?
13. How does the narrator describe the other characters? Fill in the table below to describe them.

 ISBN-978-81-8477-734-5

14. What do you know about the narrator? Add your comments to the table.

Character table	
Name/age	**Main character traits and appearance**

Vocabulary

Narratives contain both **direct** and **indirect characterisation**.

In direct characterisation, the writer **tells** the reader what is happening by making direct comments about the character. Writers often use this when they want to move on with the story and don't want to waste time. For example:

> **Ali watched as Raj placed the bag on the table, undid the clasp and opened it. There was nothing inside but scrunched-up paper!**

In indirect characterisation, the writer **shows** what the character is doing through action, speech or thoughts. Going through the following examples will show that indirect characterisation tends to involve the reader more.

 ISBN-978-81-8477-734-5

"Look," said Raj to Ali. He placed the bag on the table with a cynical little smile and undid the clasp. "There's nothing inside, but scrunched-up paper!" he announced.

Raj gave a cynical little laugh and placed the bag on the table. As he slowly opened the clasp, he was wondering what Ali would say when he discovered that there was only scrunched-up paper inside!

Indirect characterisation might also reveal what others say or how they respond to the character. For example:

"When Raj put the bag on the table and opened it," said Ali, his eyes wide with amazement, "guess what! There was nothing inside but scrunched-up paper!"

A. Is the following example from the excerpt, *Roll of Thunder, Hear My Cry*, direct or indirect characterisation?

Yet he was always sensitive to others and now, shifting the handle of his lunch can from his right hand to his right wrist and his smudged notebook from his left hand to his left armpit, he stuffed his free hands into his pockets and attempted to make his face as moody as Stacey's and as cranky as mine.

B. Choose one or more of the characters from the excerpt, *Roll of Thunder, Hear My Cry*. Write an example of direct characterisation involving the same characters and an imaginary event.

C. Now turn the example you wrote in question 2 into indirect characterisation. Remember, you can introduce new words and expressions, but you should keep the characters and events the same.

D. The following short passage is an example of indirect characterisation. Write alternative descriptions of the three characters involved, Mr Grist, Mrs Grist and the waiter, using direct characterisation.

 ISBN-978-81-8477-734-5

“The bill, sir,” said the waiter, presenting Mr Grist with a piece of paper discreetly folded in the middle.

Mr Grist unfolded the piece of paper, took out his glasses and began to examine the bill minutely.

“Shall I come back in a moment, sir?” asked the waiter.

“Be patient, if you please,” said Mr Grist, continuing his examination of the bill.

“Is anything wrong, Henry?” asked Mrs Grist. She smiled hurriedly at the waiter. “It was a very nice meal.”

“Thank you, madam,” replied the waiter with a very slight bow in Mrs Grist’s direction.

“Henry ...?” began Mrs Grist.

Mr Grist brought his eyebrows together and shot a fierce glare at his wife, who did not finish her question.

“I was just checking that our man here hadn’t charged us for your glass of water,” he said eventually. “This seems to be correct,” he added, addressing the waiter. “I suppose you’ll want to be paid.”

Mrs Grist gave the waiter another little smile, while her husband, with what sounded like a sigh of deep reluctance, reached into his jacket pocket and drew forth his wallet. He undid the clasp of his wallet, unzipped one of its pockets, pulled out two banknotes – which he rubbed together between his fingers to ensure that he was handing over two notes and not three by mistake – and deposited them on the table.

“Thank you, sir,” said the waiter. He picked up the notes and went off to the till. Mr Grist, having refastened his wallet and stowed it back in his jacket pocket, stood up to leave.

“Aren’t you going to leave a tip, dear?” asked Mrs Grist.

“Of course not,” said her husband. “The man was infernally rude!”

 ISBN-978-81-8477-734-5

Grammar

Remember that **powerful verbs** can bring a piece of writing to life. They tell us not only about what is happening, but also about how the character feels.

Other than revealing how the character feels, a verb can also add to the image of the setting. For example, if it is a warm summer day and someone is **ambling** rather than **walking**, it encourages us to sense the warmth as well as visualise the character.

A. Find the following verbs in the excerpt and make short notes in the table about how you think the character feels.

Verb	How the character feels
lagged (paragraph 2)	
threatened (paragraph 3)	
glanced (paragraph 5)	
tugged (paragraph 6)	
dragged (paragraph 6)	
imprisoned (paragraph 6)	

B. In the following exercise, write two sentences for each of the situations, choosing verbs that not only reveal how the character feels, but also add something to the setting.

 ISBN-978-81-8477-734-5

1. A character looking at snow slowly falling in the garden.

____

____

2. A character caught in a sudden summer hailstorm.

____

____

3. A tornado chaser in his car.

____

____

C. A list of powerful verbs is given in the left-hand column. Complete the meaning given in the right-hand column by adding the appropriate verb from the box.

move	grow	use up	break	check
suggest	fall down	think	turn	throw

1. creep — to ____________ quietly and inconspicuously
2. revolve — to ____________ around a central point
3. ponder — to ____________ for a long time and carefully
4. collapse — to ____________ suddenly
5. smash — to ____________ violently
6. expand — to ____________ larger
7. exhaust — to ____________ all of
8. sling — to ____________ forcefully but carelessly
9. insinuate — to ____________ in an indirect and unpleasant way
10. verify — to ____________ that something is true

 ISBN-978-81-8477-734-5

Listening

People often have different points of view about issues. Listen to these views about homework.

1. Make notes in the table about who is for or against homework.
2. Explain why, using brief notes.

Who?	For or against?	Why?
a. (an elderly man)		
b. (a mother)		
c. (a father)		
d. (a boy)		
e. (a young woman)		
f. (a female teacher)		

 ISBN-978-81-8477-734-5

Speaking

Present a short talk to a group about whether or not you think children should have homework.

1. Keep in mind the following points before you begin.
   - Refer to the views made in the section on "listening".
   - Jot down some of your own ideas.
2. Memorise your idea (you should have at least three) before presenting your talk. Try not to refer to your notes.
3. When you have finished, listen to someone who has a different point of view from yours.

Writing

Do you agree with the following statement?

Celebrities are not good role models.

1. Work with a partner. Discuss and share your ideas. You may start with thinking around the following points.
   - Who creates celebrities?
   - Why do they appeal to us?
   - Why are they often not what they seem?

 ISBN-978-81-8477-734-5

2. Complete the following "for" and "against" table on your own.

"Celebrities are not good role models."	
For	**Against**

3. Referring to your points in the table, write an argument "for" or "against" the statement.
   - In order to do this effectively, it is best to present a new paragraph for each point.
   - You should also use different kinds of connectors that help you make your point clearly and avoid contradicting yourself. For example:

Connectors of qualification	Connectors of addition
However...	In addition...
If...	As well as...
Apart from...	

4. When you have finished, read your argument to a partner and listen to his or hers.

 ISBN-978-81-8477-734-5

Activity

Add two paragraphs of your own to the excerpt from *Roll of Thunder, Hear My Cry*.

1. You can write from either:
   - Little Man's point of view, or
   - Christopher-John's point of view.

2. Remember that the children are still on the dusty road, but are approaching school.

 ISBN-978-81-8477-734-5

Theme 3

Sports

A. Look at the picture given above and answer the following questions.

1. What is the name of the sport the people in the picture are playing?
2. Do you like this sport? Give appropriate reasons for your answer.

B. Sport is an important part of people's lives. Different kinds of sport are played across the world. Answer the following questions about your preferences.

1. What is your favourite sport?
2. Why do you think sports is popular with people? What is the appeal?
3. In what way are team sports and individual sports different? Which of the two kinds do you prefer? Give reasons for your answer.

 ISBN-978-81-8477-734-5

5 The Trial

Dan Freedman is a football fan and a sports editor at the Football Association. He lives in England. This chapter is from his book, *The Kick Off*.

1 Jamie knows he has to play well in this trial match if he wants to get into the football team. But then, everything seems to go horribly wrong...

How did Jamie change throughout the story?

2 Marsden handed Jamie the ball.

3 Jamie looked around. None of the others on his team had made a move to take the penalty. It had to be him.

4 Jamie knew it wasn't just the keeper that he was up against now. It was every other player on the pitch. Not even his own teammates wanted him to score. Why would they? They all wanted to get into the A team just as badly as he did. Why would they want him to steal all the glory in the last minute?

5 Jamie reached down and placed the ball on the spot. He could feel his heart thudding as he put the ball down.

6 "Make sure you don't MISS," hissed Dillon, standing between Jamie and the goal. He was so close that Jamie could see the little droplets of spit coming out of his stinking mouth as he spoke.

Who was Dillon?

7 Jamie fended Dillon's heavy frame out of the way. He needed to concentrate. He wanted to be decisive but thousands of questions were all closing in on him at once: Power or placement? To the side? It might go wide. Straight down the middle? The keeper will save it.

 ISBN-978-81-8477-734-5

8 Mr Marsden raised the whistle to his mouth. The burst of noise was the signal for Jamie to step forward.

9 "I can't miss, I can't miss," he said to himself as he walked towards the spot, head bowed.

10 Everything went completely blank.

11 Jamie saw his feet run up to the ball but somehow felt unable to control them. His mind and body were disconnected from each other. He was taking the penalty but he had no idea what he was actually going to do with it.

12 Then, something very unlucky happened.

13 As Jamie moved to strike the ball with his left foot, his right foot went over a **divot** in the pitch, twisting his ankle right over.

---

divot: piece of loose turf

 ISBN-978-81-8477-734-5

14 It threw Jamie off balance completely. He started to fall over. He should have stopped, got himself together and taken another run-up. But he didn't. He still tried to take the penalty.

15 As he was falling, he flung his foot towards the ball so desperately, so violently, that his left boot actually flew off his foot.

16 It shot right up into the air.

17 Jamie yelled out in horror.

18 His boot rocketed skywards, doing somersaults as it went. Meanwhile, the ball that should have been flying into the back of the net was rolling slowly and painfully along the ground towards the goalkeeper's waiting hands.

19 This was his worst nightmare. All the players on both sides were laughing. At him.

20 "That's the worst penalty I've ever seen! You're rubbish!" Dillon shouted, pointing straight at Jamie.

Why were the players laughing?

21 Jamie's blood was boiling with rage, embarrassment and frustration. The sight and sound of Dillon's stupid, ugly, disgusting laugh was too much to take.

22 He shoved Dillon hard in the chest and walked away.

23 "Aaah," cried Dillon dramatically. He stumbled backwards and fell to the ground clutching his neck.

24 Jamie couldn't believe what Dillon was doing. He was actually faking it. He was pretending Jamie had punched him!

25 "Johnson, come here," said Marsden beckoning Jamie with his finger. His voice was serious.

26 "You're not falling for that, are you, sir? He's taking the –"

27 "I'm not falling for anything," Marsden reached for his pocket.

28 "Sir! I didn't do anything!"

 ISBN-978-81-8477-734-5

29 "Yes, you did, Jamie. I know you're upset about the penalty but you raised your hands to an opponent and you can't do that on a football pitch."

30 Marsden brandished the red card above his head so everyone could see.

31 Jamie had been sent off.

KINGFIELD SCHOOL			
		UNDER 14s TRIAL MATCH	
FULL-TIME RESULT			
BLUES	**1**	REDS	**0**
Walsh	12	Johnson Missed Pen. Johnson sent off	61 62

 ISBN-978-81-8477-734-5

Reading Comprehension

Answer the following questions.

Level 1

1. Why did Jamie have to play well?
2. Who handed the ball to Jamie?
3. Who threatened him?
4. What happened when Jamie moved to strike the ball?
5. What was Jamie's full name?

Level 2

6. Why is *The Trial* not an example of teamwork?
7. What does the idiom "steal the glory" mean?
8. Do you think Mr Marsden saw what happened between Jamie and Dillon? Did he act correctly?
9. How do you think Jamie felt after the game was over?
10. What lesson do you think Jamie needed to learn?

Level 3

11. Identify information in the excerpt about Jamie and Dillon, and complete the table below.

Character	What he says	What he does
Jamie		
Dillon		

 ISBN-978-81-8477-734-5

12. Use the information in the table to identify the character traits of each character.

    - Look beyond the obvious, asking yourself why the character spoke or acted as he did.
    - Use your ideas to write character sketches of Jamie and Dillon, comparing the two.

Vocabulary

Many hobbies or pursuits have their own **specific vocabulary** and **expressions**. Football is no exception. Some of these have been used in the excerpt, as shown below.

> Jamie was about to take a **penalty kick** from the **penalty box** but he couldn't decide what strategy to adopt to score a goal:
>
> He needed to concentrate. He wanted to be decisive but thousands of questions were all closing in on him at once: **Power or placement**? **To the side**? It might go wide. **Straight down the middle**? The keeper will save it.

A. Explain in your own words what do the following terms or phrases mean.

1. penalty kick
2. penalty box

 ISBN-978-81-8477-734-5

3. power or placement?
4. to the side
5. straight down the middle

B. Can you list out and explain terms or phrases used in a sport of your interest?

Example:
No-ball in cricket means an illegal delivery by a bowler.

Grammar

Adverbs can be single words or several words (these are referred to as adverbials). There are many different kinds of adverbs.

Adverbs of manner tell us **how** something was done. For example:

How did the player sneer? Aggressively

The player sneered **aggressively**.

Adverbs of time tell us **when** something was done. For example:

When did the match start? Already

The match had **already** started.

Adverbs of place tell us **where** something was done. For example:

Where did he watch the match? On his computer

He watched the match **on his computer**.

Find the adverbs of manner, time and place in the following text.

1. We all cheered madly from the sidelines. It was 2-0! Then someone pointed. Look! The referee was shouting. What was happening?

 ISBN-978-81-8477-734-5

2. It was Jerry! He was running wildly down the pitch towards the ball. We gasped as he pushed the ball backwards, forwards, sideways. Within seconds, it was in the back of the net. The crowd roared! Another goal! The referee began blowing his whistle incessantly. But Jerry took no notice. Why should he? He was only a dog.

Listening

Listen to the text about a traditional game and answer the following questions.

1. How many players are there in the game of Kho Kho and how many can play at any one time?
2. What must the players try to do?
3. Why does a player have to be athletic?
4. What do you think is "tag"?
5. When were the modern rules for Kho Kho established?

Speaking

Give a short talk to the class about a sportsperson.

1. Identify the person you want to talk about. This could be a man or a woman involved in any sport.
2. You may need to carry out some research with your teacher's guidance. Include the following:
    - Name, age, sport and the place he or she comes from.
    - When did the sportsperson begin his or her sporting career and how long has he or she been playing?
    - The skill and commitment of the sportsperson.
    - The achievements of the sportsperson.
    - Where is the sportsperson ranked in the game?

 ISBN-978-81-8477-734-5

Writing

Choose either 1 or 2 below.

1. Write a sports report. Choose a sport you know about. (This could be a sport that you enjoy or play.) Remember that sports reports often have the following features:

    - Third person past tense
    - Fast pace
    - Long sentences with lots of information, for example:

      During injury time, a header was secured by Blithers at the final against Pealby versus Overhill last Saturday at Binkerton stadium.
    - Short sharp sentences, like "rain stopped the play."

2. Write a review of a competition or contest.

    - Choose a topic that interests you (such as an art competition or a singing, dancing or theatrical performance).
    - Mention who the main contestants are along with some details (these should be imaginary).
    - Make notes about each of the contestants, using the following table:

Contestant	Strength	Weakness	Any other point

 ISBN-978-81-8477-734-5

Activity

What do you think is the best way to carry out a successful penalty kick?

1. Write an eight to ten-point plan explaining this.
2. Remember the following points.
   - the frame of mind you should adopt
   - the physical skills needed
   - the judgements you should make
   - how to behave after you have kicked the ball

 ISBN-978-81-8477-734-5

6 The Spirit of Cricket

Sunil Gavaskar is a former cricketer and captain of the Indian cricket team. He has written four books on cricket – *Sunny Days, Idols, Runs n' Ruins* and *One Day Wonders*. The following speech is from the MCC Spirit of Cricket Cowdrey Lecture delivered on 29 July 2003.

1 Will we ever get the likes of Sir Garfield Sobers and G. R. Vishwanath again? That greatest of cricketers, Gary Sobers, not only indicated more than once to umpires that he had caught the ball on the bounce but also declared his innings closed once in a test match in spite of having two of his main bowlers injured and left a challenging target. If a captain does that today, of course, the Anti-corruption Unit of the ICC would be breathing down his neck, but all Gary wanted was to enliven a dead series.

What tone does the author adopt in his speech?

2 G. R. Vishwanath was the captain who recalled Bob Taylor when he was given out by the umpire. Bob's bat had brushed the pads, which had misled the umpire into giving him out caught behind. Like the true sportsman he is, Vishy walked up to the umpire and politely withdrew the appeal. India lost the test, but Vishy is remembered for that and loved all the more for it.

3 Today, thanks to the win-at-all-costs theory, appeals are made even though the fielders know that the batsman is not out. There is the other side, of course, where a batsman knows he is out but stays put and rubs some other part of his body if it's an appeal for a catch or shows his bat if there's an appeal for lbw. The rewards

How does he compare the present with the past as far as cricket is concerned?

 ISBN-978-81-8477-734-5

have become high, and rightly so, but it has to a great extent taken away from the spirit of the game, where bowlers applauded a good shot and batsmen acknowledged with a nod a good delivery from a bowler who beat them. While today, in order not to give any psychological advantage to the opposition, there's hardly any applause from the fielding side when a batsman reaches a fifty or a century.

4 It's hard to understand how applauding **concedes** any advantage to the batsman, but we see it increasingly where, barring the odd fielder, the others feign total ignorance of the batsman reaching a landmark.

5 This is in stark contrast to my first series in the West Indies, where one could sit with the greats like Gary Sobers, Rohan Kanhai and Lance Gibbs at the end of a day's play and ask them about batting and how to improve. They were more than happy to give good sound advice, even though it was to an opponent and could be used against them the next day to their team's **detriment**. It wasn't that these great cricketers did not want their team to win. It was just the fact that they believed that helping an opponent only produced good cricket and was good for the game.

6 How about the England team under Norman Yardley raising three cheers for Don Bradman when he came out to play his last test innings? Such a gesture is unthinkable today, where the opponents hardly greet each other and if there's anything to say it's invariably not very pleasant. The thinking is that with the stakes being so high, any friendly overture takes away from the competitiveness of the player.

7 Today, though there is a Code of Conduct, the verbal bouncers go on pretty much unchecked and, unless something is done quickly about it, the good name of the game that we all know will be mud. Just look at any school game anywhere in the world and we will see bowlers having a go at the batsman. They see their heroes doing it on TV and believe that it is a part of the game, and so indulge in it.

---

concedes: grants, allows
detriment: loss, disadvantage

 ISBN-978-81-8477-734-5

8 Here, it is crucial for the coaches to step in and tell them, while the kids are at an impressionable age, that this is wrong and that cricket has been played for years without indulging in personal abuse. Maybe we should tell TV producers that, just like they don't show any of the streakers at the ground anymore, they should not show close-ups of players verbalising each other. With the cameras being so good, it is easy to lip-read and kids can see that it is not the Bible nor the Koran nor the (Bhagvad) Gita which is being quoted on the field.

9 The sad part is that very little is being done about it. If a player even so much as glares at the umpire or stays a micro-second longer at the crease after being given out, he is hauled up and is in trouble. If there is protection for the umpire from the players, why not protection to players from abusive players?

10 ... Let me end by repeating part of what Sir Don Bradman said about the game. We are all custodians of the game, and the game will prosper if we can leave it better than we found it. It is something that we must all endeavour to do – and it is achievable if we work sincerely towards it. I am confident that we can do it and when – and not if – we do it, then Colin [Cowdrey] sitting up there with the gods will smile and say, "Well done, chaps – that's the spirit."

 ISBN-978-81-8477-734-5

Reading Comprehension

A. Answer the following questions.

Level 1

1. Who is Sunil Gavaskar?
2. Where is the extract from?
3. Who does the author remember with respect and affection?

Level 2

4. What does "If a captain does that today, the Anti-corruption Unit of the ICC would be breathing down his neck" mean?
5. Why was the umpire misled?
6. What does the "win-at-all-costs" theory mean and how does it affect the game of cricket? Do you think that this theory is applicable in any other sport? Which sport do you think is affected by this theory and why?
7. When would it be appropriate for the opposition to applaud a player and why does this no longer take place?
8. What do you think "the spirit of cricket" should be?

B. The excerpt below gives a mix of fact and opinion. Read it and answer the questions.

Level 3

This is in stark contrast to my first series in the West Indies, where one could sit with the greats like Gary Sobers, Rohan Kanhai and Lance Gibbs at the end of a day's play and ask them about batting and how to improve. They were more than happy to give good sound advice, even though it was to an opponent and could be used against them the next day to their team's detriment. It wasn't that these great cricketers did not want their team to win. It was just the fact that they believed that helping an opponent only produced good cricket and was good for the game.

 ISBN-978-81-8477-734-5

9. Underline the facts in the above passage in one colour and opinions in a different one.

10. Complete the table by making short notes about facts and opinions in the correct column.

11. Make sure that you select your points carefully!

The Spirit of Cricket	
Facts	**Opinions**

C. Read the following comment.

How about the England team under Norman Yardley raising three cheers for Don Bradman when he came out to play his last test innings? Such a gesture is unthinkable today where the opponents hardly greet each other...

12. From your knowledge of sport, do you agree with the opinion expressed about cricket (or sport in general) today? Write a paragraph to explain.

 ISBN-978-81-8477-734-5

Vocabulary

Cricket has complicated and strange vocabulary. **Cricketing terms** are unique and meanings cannot be guessed from the individual words such as **lbw**, **bouncer** etc.

A. Match each cricketing term on the left with its meaning on the right.

Term	Meaning
deep	can bat as well as bowl
a century	when the bat is held with a light grip and the ball loses speed and falls to the ground
a dead bat	when the ball bounces more than twice or rolls along the pitch
all-rounder	the part of the field that is near the boundary point
daisy cutter	a hundred runs

B. Work in pairs and find the meanings of the following terms.

- caught behind (paragraph 2)
- lbw (paragraph 3)

Find out what they mean. Take it in turns to explain to your partner!

 ISBN-978-81-8477-734-5

C. Different sports use different methods of scoring to decide who wins and who loses. Insert the correct "score word" into the gaps in the following sentences. To help you, the name of the relevant sport appears in brackets at the end of the sentence.

1. Murray won the first set by six ___________ to four. (Tennis)
2. Ravi was unable to knock his opponent out, but won the fight on ___________. (Boxing)
3. At the end of their first innings, Pakistan have a lead of 114 ___________. (Cricket)
4. Our school team scored three ___________ in the second half. (Hockey)
5. New Zealand won the game by a single ___________. (Rugby)
6. Soraya is two ___________ behind the leader. (Golf)

Grammar

In English, nouns usually have the **definite article**, **the**, and the **indefinite articles**, **a** and **an**.

However, sometimes we don't have to use an article and we call this the **zero article**. For example, we don't have to use it with uncountable nouns, or before names of people, places or languages.

I love sports.

The cricket team is from India.

Padma speaks English perfectly.

 ISBN-978-81-8477-734-5

We can also drop the article with plural nouns when writing or discussing things in general.

The competitors gathered in their teams.

Or

Competitors love the challenge.

A. Write sentences of your own with the following words.

cricketers pitch Mumbai exercise umpire fans spectacle game

1. Think whether or not you could use the definite, indefinite or zero article.
2. You could include more than one example in a single sentence if you wished.
3. You could also write a paragraph using the words as part of a topic.

B. Decide whether the blanks in the following sentences should be filled with the definite article (**the**), the indefinite article (**a / an**), or be left unfilled. Put a cross (**X**) in the blank if it should be left unfilled.

1. Have you found _____ book that you were looking for yet?
2. No, I don't want _____ milk in my tea, thank you.
3. Is there _____ pen that I could borrow?
4. Ravi arrived today on _____ 10.30 flight from _____ Sri Lanka.
5. Do you eat this dish with _____ rice or with _____ bread?
6. She's eating her soup with _____ wrong spoon!
7. To make this dish, you will need _____ onion, _____ clove of garlic, 250 grams of _____ minced lamb and 100 millilitres of _____ water.

 ISBN-978-81-8477-734-5

8. Milly wants to study _____ geography at _____ university.

9. To reduce _____ risk of _____ accident, _____ high-visibility clothing should be worn at all times.

10. It takes _____ skill and _____ patience to create _____ complex work of art.

Listening

Listen to the text about Dilip Doshi and answer the following questions.

1. When was Dilip Doshi born?
2. When did he reach the height of his career?
3. Who is Nayan Doshi and where was he born?
4. Why might the saying "like father like son" apply here?
5. In what way is Nayan's situation different from his father's?

 ISBN-978-81-8477-734-5

Speaking

What physical exercise do you do to keep yourself fit? Which sports do you play in school? What sport do you enjoy the best? Do you play it regularly or are you just a fan?

Perhaps neither do you enjoy any sport nor are you a fan of any.

Choose from the questions above and use them as a guide to present a talk about sport to a small group.

1. Give your talk an interesting title.
2. Begin by giving a brief introduction to your talk.

Writing

Refer to the speech, *The Spirit of Cricket*, and the related exercises in the section "Reading Comprehension" and decide which opinion you most agree with.

1. Write about 450 words explaining why you think sport is important to young people in general.
2. Take into account the author's views on the effects of television and whether or not you agree with them.
3. Draw on your own experience of sport or contests of any kind, as well as the speech to support your opinions.

 ISBN-978-81-8477-734-5

Activity

Write a ten-point code of behaviour for a game or sport. It could be for cricket or any other sport. Consider the following:

1. Teamwork
2. How do the players regard the other team
3. How do the teams regard the crowd / fans
4. How do individual players behave
5. How the game can become exciting and entertaining

You could use the following introductory words:

Always...

Remember...

Never...

 ISBN-978-81-8477-734-5

Theme 4

Our views

A. Look at the picture above and answer the following questions.

1. Where is the revolving door located?
2. Why do some places use revolving doors?
3. Do you think children will enjoy revolving doors? Why or why not?

B. Did you like riding on escalators or elevators when you were small? Describe your response to them.

 ISBN-978-81-8477-734-5

7 Elevators and Escalators

Read the following poem by Sampurna Chattarji about elevators and escalators.

In what way does the poet treat escalators and elevators?

1 Elevators and Escalators are cousins.
Elevators like listening to music.
Escalators don't.

2 Elevators are moody, they break down.
Sometimes the old ones – the ones
with the grille doors – get stuck between floors.
In movies, it's always the Elevator
that comes crashing down a zillion storeys,
ending in explosions of electricity and toasted hair.

3 And Escalators?

Escalators purr smoothly up and down,
secretly sticking out their tongues at their cranky, noisy,
disaster-prone, twice-removed cousins.

4 Elevators have men to run them.
The men sit on stools in uniforms
and press the buttons smartly
every time someone goes up or down.

5 Escalators are lonely.
No one runs them. They run on their own,
up and down, endlessly.
Escalators hate Elevators
when it comes to the question of men.

 ISBN-978-81-8477-734-5

6 Escalators know that there are two kinds
of humans on this planet.
The ones who are cowards
and the ones who are brave.

7 The brave ones *always* take the Escalator.

The scaredy-cats take the Elevator, not daring
to put their feet on the running treads,
they *dread* the fact that Escalators *never* stop,
except at night, when the malls are closed,
and even then they run, endlessly,
in the nightmares of the Elevator-people.

What images in particular come to mind as you read the poem?

8 Escalators sneer at the Elevator-people.

Escalators are smooth and sly
and love those who love to glide,
love pointy painted toes,
love hems of shiny silk,
love soft and brushing hands.

9 Elevators are private. They hate crowds.
Takes only sixteen, you moron!, they want to say
to the seventeenth person who squeezes in at the very last moment.

10 The Elevator's dearest wish is to be empty all day,
with no one but a little boy for company,
tall enough on tiptoe to reach the highest button,
small enough to know that riding up and down
is their shared idea of heaven.

 ISBN-978-81-8477-734-5

Reading Comprehension

A. Answer the following questions.

Level 1

1. In what sense are elevators moody?
2. What animal comes to your mind at the mention of escalators in verse 3?
3. Which one is lonely – elevators or escalators? Why?
4. Why might people be frightened of escalators?
5. In the poem, which gets stuck – elevators or escalators?

Level 2

6. Why do you think elevators like listening to music, while escalators don't?
7. The poet says that the "brave" always take the escalator. But in what sense is it true that those who take the elevator are braver?

 ISBN-978-81-8477-734-5

8. From what perspective is the poet looking when she describes "pointy painted toes" and "hems of shiny silk"?

9. Why does the elevator come a little closer to heaven?

10. Why do you think elevators in particular feature in films? Search for clues in the poem.

Level 3

11. Based on your reading of the poem, contrast the escalator and the elevator as the poet sees them.
    - Write two paragraphs.
    - Use appropriate connectives as shown in the following example.

Connectors of contrast
Instead...
Unlike...

12. Do you think the escalator and elevator are similar in any way? Add comments to suggest why. Use appropriate connectives in your answer as shown in the following example.

Connectors of comparison
As with...
Similarly...

 ISBN-978-81-8477-734-5

Vocabulary

Can you remember what alliteration is? **Alliteration** is the repeated use of a particular letter or sound at the beginning of a number of words in a sentence.

Look at these examples:

silently **s**lipping away	*The "s" creates a soft or hissing sound.*
Escalators and **E**levators	*The repetition of "e" (through the poem) re-inforces the sound.*

You can use sounds in all kinds of ways in poetry. Some of the well-known tongue twisters have alliterations in plenty. For example:

Betty **b**ought **b**utter **b**ut the **b**utter was **b**itter, so **B**etty **b**ought **b**etter **b**utter to make the **b**itter **b**utter **b**etter.

Wayne **w**ent to **W**ales to **w**atch **w**alruses.

When vowel sounds are repeated, we call this **assonance**:

p**ee**ling p**ea**ches

Did you notice that "**p**eeling **p**eaches" also includes alliteration? Another example of assonance is from one of the advertising slogans from 1950s about vacuum cleaners:

It b**ea**ts... as it sw**ee**ps... as it cl**ea**ns!

A. Based on your reading of the poem, answer the following questions.

1. Find examples of alliteration and assonance in the first two verses of the poem *Elevators and Escalators*.
2. Discuss with a partner what effect these sounds create in the poem.
3. Are you familiar with the ensuing tongue twisters? They are full of alliteration and assonance as well as repetition of other sounds. Can you identify the alliterations and assonances?

 ISBN-978-81-8477-734-5

- Peter Piper picked a peck of pickled pepper.
  If Peter Piper picked a peck of pickled pepper,
  Where's the peck of pickled pepper Peter Piper picked?
- Denise sees the fleece,
  Denise sees the fleas.
  At least Denise could sneeze
  and feed and freeze the fleas.

4. Create some comic rhyming couplets (two lines) using alliteration and assonance.

1.	Birdie birdie in the sky laid a turdie in my eye. If cows could fly I'd have a cow pie in my eye.
2.	______________________________ ______________________________
3.	______________________________ ______________________________

 ISBN-978-81-8477-734-5

B. Alliteration and assonance are perhaps most often used in poetry. Read the following excerpt from the poem *Spring* by Gerard Manley Hopkins. Try to identify as many instances of alliteration and assonance as you can.

Nothing is so beautiful as spring –
    When weeds in wheels shoot long and lovely and lush;
    Thrush's eggs look little low heavens, and thrush
Through the echoing timber does so rinse and wring
The ear, it strikes like lightnings to hear him sing;
    The glassy peartree leaves and blooms, they brush
    The descending blue; that blue is all in a rush
With richness; the racing lambs too have fair their fling.

Grammar

Adjectives are formed in many ways by **adding suffixes**. Look at the following examples.

Root words	*Adjectives*
wood →	wood**en** wood**ed** wood**y**
music →	music**al**

 ISBN-978-81-8477-734-5

A. Look at the root words given below. How many different adjectives can you make by adding suffixes from the box? Remember that you may have to change the spelling of the root word before adding the suffix.

-able -ed -ful -less -ly -ous -y

Root words	Adjectives
joy	
lone	
love	
mood	
noise	
point	
use	
class	
taste	
hope	
tire	

 ISBN-978-81-8477-734-5

B. Create adjectives with the opposite meaning to the adjectives listed below by adding the appropriate prefixes from the box.

dis-	il-	im-	in-	un-

1. tolerable ____________________
2. patient ____________________
3. ready ____________________
4. sufficient ____________________
5. liberal ____________________

Listening

Listen to the text about elevators and answer the following questions.

1. When might the first elevator have been created?
2. In what were winches or hoists used and why?

 ISBN-978-81-8477-734-5

3. Which is the tallest building in the world?

4. How long does it take to travel 124 floors in that building?

Speaking

Some people find elevators disturbing and claustrophobic. Others find escalators disturbing and prefer stairs as they are static. What are your views?

1. Has any dangerous thing happened to you on an escalator or in an elevator?
2. Refer back to the work done so far and make your notes.
3. Then give a talk to a partner about either escalators or elevators or both. You might include your preference as one of the points in the talk.

Writing

Create a shape poem, also known as theme poem, about either an escalator or an elevator.

1. Write the poem first. It doesn't have to rhyme.
2. Think carefully about the shape that an elevator or an escalator makes. Try writing shape words first. Some examples are given below for your help.

p s

e t

e a

t i u

dr p s r b mp

o

 ISBN-978-81-8477-734-5

3. Now draw the shape of an escalator or an elevator.

Remember

- Keep your pictures simple.
- The picture should not become more important than the words.

Activity

Find out about the Paternoster elevator.

1. Find out the following information.
    - Where does the name Paternoster come from? What does it mean?
    - How does it work?
    - What are the dangers associated with it? Why is it considered unsafe?
    - What else can you find out about it?
2. Write an account using the information you have.
3. Include a diagram in your account to show the following.
    - How the elevator works
    - How it is different from the conventional elevator

 ISBN-978-81-8477-734-5

8 Shrek: A Review

Read the following review about all the Shrek films by Mary Green.

1 The Shrek films, based on William Steig's picture book by the same name, have been hugely popular during the last ten years or so. Most of us are familiar with the ogre hero and his Princess Fiona of Far Far Away. Princess Fiona is strong (and more confident than Shrek), has her own opinions and is pretty good at martial arts. The films have been shown worldwide and audiences everywhere seem to have a similar response to it.

? What does the introductory paragraph tell you?

2 The first film, *Shrek* (2001), was well received by the critics and had a huge collection at the box office. Keen to make money, plans for *Shrek 2* were soon on the table and the film was equally well received in 2004. The critics felt that the humour was spot on and universal. It takes a jab at celebrity culture and also the traditional fairy tale by presenting an untypical hero – a giant – and a feisty princess. Most felt that the computer animation was

? What sort of tense is used in the passage, present or past?

 ISBN-978-81-8477-734-5

inspiring and likewise the characters. Both major and minor characters were regarded as engaging and original. Donkey is Shrek's side-kick and has some brilliant lines, particularly in his bickering exchanges.

3 By contrast, *Shrek the Third* (2007) is largely viewed as disappointing. Shrek is in danger of becoming king, a responsibility he doesn't want. So, along with Donkey and Puss in Boots, he sets off to find the suitable person to be the king, but the plot never really gets going. Instead of a witty dialogue, the script seems tired. Many of the jokes are unoriginal and the characters seem to run out of steam, unlike their antics in the first two films, which always kept the audience entertained.

4 The fourth film, *Shrek Forever After* (2010), seems to be back on form. It has been a commercial success, with box office collection going up and critics generally in agreement that it is more engaging and much better than *Shrek the Third*.

Reading Comprehension

A. Answer the following questions based on your reading of the review.

Level 1

1. Who wrote the book, *Shrek*? What type of a book is it?
2. Where does Princess Fiona come from?
3. When were *Shrek*, *Shrek 2* and *Shrek the Third* released?
4. Why did plans to make *Shrek 2* get underway quickly?

Level 2

5. In what way is Shrek an untypical hero?
6. In what way is Princess Fiona not a typical princess from a fairy tale?
7. What does the expression "take a jab at celebrity culture" mean?
8. What do the critics mean when they say the humour in these films is "universal"?

 ISBN-978-81-8477-734-5

9. Why do you think *Shrek the Third* was less successful and "tired"?

10. What happened to the series by 2010?

11. What was the opinion of the critics about the last installment from the Shrek franchise?

B. Read about the connectors of comparison and contrast, and answer the following questions.

Level 3

In the first paragraph, the connector of comparison "**in much the same way**" is used to show similarity.

Paragraph 3 starts with a connector of contrast "**by contrast**" to show difference.

12. What other examples of connectors of comparison and connectors of contrast can you find in the passage? Complete the table below.

Connectors	
Comparison	**Contrast**

13. Choose one from each column in the table above to write a sentence about *Shrek*, showing similarity and difference.

 ISBN-978-81-8477-734-5

Vocabulary

There are several expressions which show that the review is written in an **informal style**.

A. Some of the informal expressions used in the review are listed here along with similar expressions that have different meanings. Do you know what they mean? Write their meaning in the table.

Expression	Meaning
pretty good	
pretty much	
on the table	
under the table	
at the box office	
think out of the box	
spot on	
blind spot	
run out of steam	
full steam ahead	
back on form	
back off	

 ISBN-978-81-8477-734-5

B. Match the following expressions in column A with the ones in column B having similar meaning.

A	Similar expression
spot on	mote in one's eye
pretty good	give up
on the table	burn out
blind spot	well done
back off	quite well
run out of steam	table that thought

C. Write a diary entry (about 200 words) in informal style about your surprise at finding something important or visiting somewhere special.

Begin:

7 July

I couldn't believe my luck today!

 ISBN-978-81-8477-734-5

Grammar

We use **comparatives** when we want to compare one thing with another, usually by adding **-er** to an adjective.

To compare three things or more, we can use the **superlative** form by adding "est". See the example given below.

a **fast** runner, a **faster** runner, the **fastest** runner

With some adjectives, usually longer words, we use "more" to form the comparative and "most" to form the superlative. See the example given below.

more generous, **most** generous

For some adjectives, the comparative and superlative forms look very different from the adjective. See the example given below.

good, **better**, **best**

A. Complete the table below.

Adjective	Comparative	Superlative
flat		
large		
heavy		
busy		
wide		
fit		

 ISBN-978-81-8477-734-5

B. Write down the comparatives and superlatives of the following adjectives. Add them to the table below.

Adjective	Comparative	Superlative
bad		
little		
many		
much		

C. Find two examples of comparison in *Shrek: A Review*.

Remember

Don't use "more" or "less" with an adjective that is a comparative.

D. Fill in each gap in the passage with a word from the box.

elastic	elder	older	enough	ball	none
longer	most popular	smaller	most exciting	big	

(Note: There are more gaps than there are words in the box. In order to complete the passage, you may use the same word from the box as many times as it is required.)

It was the ______________ day of the year for the people in the village, especially the children. The circus was coming!

Every year the circus arrived in late spring, shortly before the human and animal performers took a well-earned summer break. Every year,

 ISBN-978-81-8477-734-5

it brought the same performers. They might be getting a little _______________, but they seemed to have lost _______________ of their flair and agility – though Yasmina and her _______________ sister Yamuna, the trapeze artists, no _______________ performed without a safety net.

Still the _______________ artiste in the show, as far as most people were concerned, was Rupesh, the amazing rubber man. He was just as _______________ as he had been 40 years before when he had first appeared in the show as a teenager. He could still fold himself up _______________ and _______________ until he could fit inside a little suitcase just _______________ enough to hold an overcoat. He could still stretch his arm out _______________ and _______________ until he could reach over his shoulder and down his back far _______________ to smack himself on the behind. And when he rolled himself up into a _______________ and started to bounce about the ring, none of the clowns could catch him even now.

 ISBN-978-81-8477-734-5

Listening

Listen to the text and answer the following questions.

1. How old was the writer when he saw his first 3D movie?
2. What was the colour of the glasses that he had to wear?
3. What effect did 3D give?
4. What method was used to create 3D?
5. What else can create 3D effects?
6. When were 3D effects first created?
7. What is 4D?

Speaking

Choose two movies that you have seen to compare and contrast.

1. Consider the following before you choose. The films could:
    - have similar characters (such as young people), but have a very different style (such as a thriller and a comedy)
    - have characters that are quite different, but are similar in style
    - use different techniques (such as 3D and conventional filming)
2. Present a speech which draws out the similarities and differences between the two films.
3. Finish your speech by saying which film you enjoyed the most. Also, do mention the reason for your preference.

 ISBN-978-81-8477-734-5

Writing

Write a film review of a current television programme (such as a comedy show) you have seen.

1. Keep the following points in mind while writing the review.
    - Give brief information about the characters and other features.
    - Express your opinions clearly saying why you like / dislike the programme.
    - Use a chatty, friendly style.
    - Use the present tense.
    - Draw comparisons with another programme, saying which is better (for example, another comedy).
    - Use comparisons and connectors to help you write clearly.
    - Use the past tense if you refer to another past programme.
2. Study the text below before you begin.

connector of contrast

By contrast, *Shrek the Third* (2007) is largely viewed as disappointing. **Shrek is in danger of becoming king, a responsibility he doesn't want**. So, along with Donkey and Puss in Boots, he sets off to find the suitable person to be the king, but the plot never really gets going. Instead of a witty dialogue, **the script seems tired**. Many of the jokes are unoriginal and the characters seem to run out of steam, unlike their antics in the first two films, which always kept the audience entertained.

information on the plot

opinion criticising film

The fourth film, *Shrek Forever After* (2010) seems to be **back on form**. It has been a commercial success, with box office takings up and critics generally in agreement that it is more engaging and **much better** than *Shrek the Third*.

informal, chatty style

comparison

 ISBN-978-81-8477-734-5

Activity

A storyboard is a series of illustrations created in sequence and is used to show the storyline or action of a film.

Create your own storyboard of frames for a simple animation.

1. Think of your own idea or choose from the following:
   - Dog wagging its tail
   - Hippopotamus yawning
   - Diver diving into a pool
   - Dancer leaping and landing
   - Bird flying
   - Blooming rose
   - A school kid
   - Fisherman and his fishing line

 ISBN-978-81-8477-734-5

2. Use the storyboard boxes given below.

 ISBN-978-81-8477-734-5

Theme 5

Relations

Look at the picture above and answer the following questions.

1. Who is the oldest member of the family?
2. Who is the youngest?
3. Can you see any members of the family that look particularly like each other?
4. How many generations do you think there are?
5. Do you prefer a large or a small family? Why or why not?

  ISBN-978-81-8477-734-5

9 Brother and Sister

Read the following poem.

1 "SISTER, sister, go to bed!
Go and rest your weary head."
Thus the **prudent** brother said.

2 "Do you want a battered hide,
Or scratches to your face applied?"
Thus his sister calm replied.

3 "Sister, do not raise my **wrath**.
I'd make you into mutton **broth**
As easily as kill a moth."

4 The sister raised her beaming eye
And looked on him **indignantly**
And sternly answered, "Only try!"

5 Off to the cook he quickly ran.
"Dear Cook, please lend a frying pan
To me as quickly as you can."

---

prudent: sensible, wise
wrath: anger
broth: soup
indignantly: crossly

 ISBN-978-81-8477-734-5

6 “And **wherefore** should I lend it you?”
“The reason, Cook, is plain to view.
I wish to make an Irish **stew**.”

7 “What meat is in that stew to go?”
“My sister'll be the contents!”
“Oh!”
“You'll lend the pan to me, Cook?”
“No!”

Moral: Never stew your sister.

Reading Comprehension

A. Answer the following questions.

Level 1

1. What does the brother want his sister to do in verse 1?
2. How does the sister react to her brother's demand?
3. What does the boy threaten to do to make his sister go to bed?
4. What does the brother want from the cook?
5. How does the cook react?

Level 2

6. The poet uses the words “prudent” and “calm”. Do you think the poet is being serious?
7. What is the boy's attitude to his sister? Explain your answer.
8. What are the sister's character traits? List some words that describe her.

---

wherefore: why, for what reason
stew: meat and vegetables cooked slowly in a pot

 ISBN-978-81-8477-734-5

B. The poem, *Brother and Sister*, ends with a moral. Read the poem again and answer the following questions.

Level 3

9. What is a moral?
10. Why is the moral of this poem absurd?
11. Why do you think the poet has included a moral at the end of this poem?
12. Find another example in this book of a story that has a moral.

Vocabulary

Onomatopoeia refers to words that sound like their meaning. The word "onomatopoeia" means making of a name or word that mimics the sound being uttered or spoken. For example, the word **Oh** in the last verse signals surprise by the cook. It mirrors the sound of surprise.

The word **battered** (verse 2) has onomatopoeic qualities since its sound reminds the reader of a hit or strike. The following words, which might be onomatopoeic, are associated with the word "battered".

Bash! **Bam!** **Whack!**

 ISBN-978-81-8477-734-5

Some more examples of frequently used words are listed below:

Warning ⟶ **Beep**
Interjecting ⟶ **Achoo**
Tweet ⟶ **Chirp**

A. What onomatopoeic words can you think of that might express the meaning of the following. Complete the table.

Word	Onomatopoeia
someone being cross	
a hot day	
a cat scratching	
an angry dog	
someone eating	
an old car	
someone laughing	
explosion	

 ISBN-978-81-8477-734-5

B. The following short poem is by Robert Browning. It is called *Meeting At Night*. It contains two notable examples of onomatopoeia. Try to identify them.

The grey sea and the long black land;
And the yellow half-moon large and low;
And the startled little waves that leap
In fiery **ringlets** from their sleep,
As I gain the cove with pushing **prow**,
And **quench** its speed **i'** the slushy sand.

Then a mile of warm sea-scented beach;
Three fields to cross till a farm appears;
A tap at the pane, the quick sharp scratch
And blue spurt of a lighted match,
And a voice less loud, through its joys and fears,
Than the two hearts beating each to each!

---

ringlets: small rings or ring-shaped objects, especially small curls or spiral of hair
prow: pointed front end of a boat
quench: extinguish or stop it
"i'": it is the shortened form of "in"

 ISBN-978-81-8477-734-5

Grammar

The **infinitive** is the basic form of a verb. It has several features and can be used in many ways as shown in the example below.

"And wherefore should I **lend** it you?"
"The reason, Cook, is plain to **view**."

Some of the features of the infinitive are listed here:

- It frequently has "to" in front of it. For example:
  My sister likes **to eat** spicy food.
- It comes after some nouns or pronouns.
- It comes after "wh" words (such as "who" and "which") and "how".
- It can be used with a modal verb, in which case the "to" is dropped. For example:
  Although Mr Goyal spent an extra class period helping us **understand** logarithms, we still bombed the test.

A. Underline the infinitives in the following paragraph.

Fahad's younger sister Parvati wanted to go to the match. Mum said she could, providing Fahad agreed to keep Parvati from getting into trouble. Fahad moaned. He couldn't decide what to do. So, Mum said they should take a packed lunch to eat. This cheered up Fahad, who said he would take care of his naughty sister, but only if Mum promised to include his favourite food – samosas.

B. Work in pairs and explain how the infinitives you have underlined are used.

 ISBN-978-81-8477-734-5

C. The following sentences require a noun that can be followed by an infinitive. Fill in each blank with a noun from the box.

(Note: You do not need to use all the words in the box. Find six words that can be followed by an infinitive and that make sense in these sentences.)

answer	decisions	drink	food	order	patience
plans	solution	strength	thought	way	weakness

1. There must be a ____________ to switch the machine off, mustn't there?
2. I'd like a nice cool ____________ to quench my thirst.
3. She barely had the ____________ to lift her arm up off the bed.
4. We received an ____________ to advance five kilometres further down the road.
5. At present, we have no ____________ to build on this site.
6. I hope that he has the ____________ to wait for a better opportunity.

Listening

Listen to the riddle carefully. Can you work out who "that man" is?

 ISBN-978-81-8477-734-5

Speaking

Discuss in groups of four the value of family life and some of the difficulties that brothers and sisters experience. Make notes in the table below.

Values	Difficulties

1. Report your discussion to another group and also listen to their views.
2. Appoint someone to make notes.
3. Appoint someone to report to the other group.

 ISBN-978-81-8477-734-5

Writing

Write your own poem about an imaginary relative.

1. Make your character eccentric or comic in some way.
2. Try to make your poem rhyme, but make sure it isn't forced.
3. If you find it difficult to rhyme successfully, write in free verse.
4. Before you begin, jot down some ideas about your character using the spider diagram. When you have decided on a name, write it in the centre. Make notes on the following characteristics.
   - Their age
   - Their appearance
   - What makes them eccentric
   - An unusual job or hobby they have
   - The kind of things they say (perhaps they have a familiar expression that they often repeat)
   - Anything else you consider is important

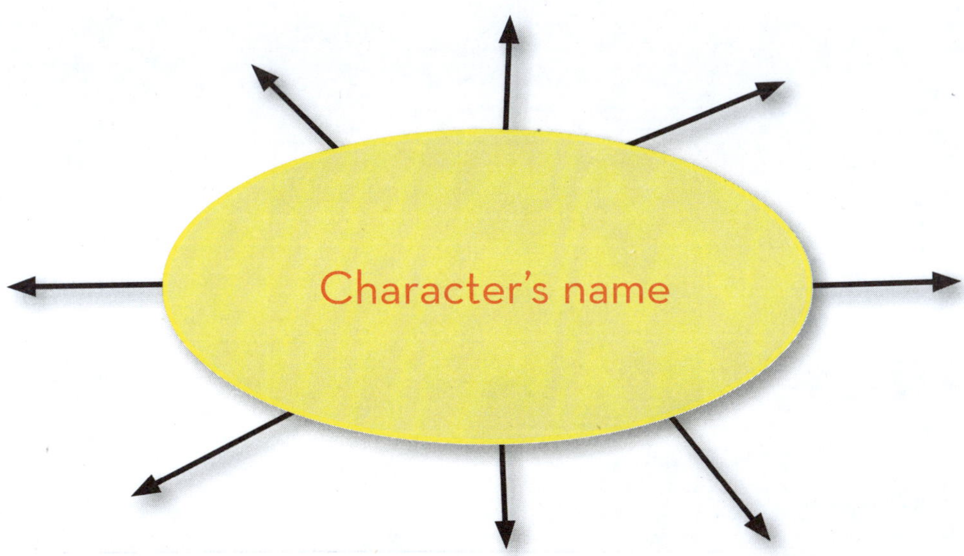

 ISBN-978-81-8477-734-5

Activity

A. Based on your experience of the group discussion in the section on "Speaking", work with a member of the group to create a ten-point code for discussions. (The remaining students in the group should also work in pairs.)

1. You should think about how you personally conduct yourself and also how the group can work together successfully. Examples are given for you to start with. Write the remaining points on paper.

Ten-point code
i) Everyone in the group should be given the opportunity to express their opinion.
ii) Try to speak clearly and coherently.
iii)
iv)
v)
vi)
vii)
viii)
ix)
x)

 ISBN-978-81-8477-734-5

2. When you complete your code, share it with the group as a whole. In between, combine your codes, rejecting some points and keeping others, so that you end up with a final, re-drafted ten points as a group.

B. Work with your group to find out who composed the poem *Brother and Sister*. With your teacher's assistance, you may search on the Internet.

C. While doing your research, find out some more funny poems on the relationship shared between siblings.

 ISBN-978-81-8477-734-5

10 Skellig

Read the first chapter from the novel *Skellig* by David Almond.

Chapter One

1 I found him in the garage on a Sunday afternoon. It was the day after we moved into Falconer Road. The winter was ending. Mum had said we'd be moving just in time for the spring. Nobody else was there. Just me. The others were inside the house with Doctor Death, worrying about the baby.

2 He was lying there in the darkness behind the tea chests, in the dust and dirt. It was as if he'd been there forever. He was filthy and pale and dried out, and I thought he was dead. I couldn't have been more wrong. I'd soon begin to see the truth about him, that there'd never been another creature like him in the world.

3 We called it the garage because that's what the estate agent, Mr Stone, called it. It was more like a demolition site or a rubbish dump or like one of those ancient warehouses they keep pulling down at the quay. Stone led us down the garden, tugged the door open and shone his little torch into the gloom. We shoved our heads in at the doorway with him.

 ISBN-978-81-8477-734-5

4 "You have to see it with your mind's eye," he said. "See it cleaned, with new doors and the roof repaired. See it as a wonderful two-car garage."

5 He looked at me with a stupid grin on his face.

6 "Or something for you, lad – a hideaway for you and your mates. What about that, eh?"

7 I looked away. I didn't want anything to do with him. All the way round the house, it had been the same. Just see it in your mind's eye. Just imagine what could be done. All the way round, I kept thinking of the old man, Ernie Myers, that had lived here on his own for years. He's been dead nearly a week before they found him under the table in the kitchen. That's what I saw when Stone told us about seeing with the mind's eye. He even said it when we got to the dining room and there was an old cracked toilet sitting there in the corner behind a plywood screen. I just wanted him to shut up, but he whispered that towards the end, Ernie couldn't manage the stairs. His bed was brought in here and a toilet was put in so everything was easy for him. Stone looked at me like he didn't think I should know about such things. I wanted to get out, to get back to our old house again, but Mum and Dad took it all in. They went on like it was going to be some big adventure. They bought the house. They started cleaning it and scrubbing it and painting it. Then the baby came too early. And here we were.

Reading Comprehension

A. Answer the following questions.

Level 1

1. Where is the story set in?
2. What time of year was it when the family moved in?
3. In what person is the story told, and who is the narrator?
4. What does the narrator call the "garage"?

 ISBN-978-81-8477-734-5

Level 2

5. What do you think the narrator has found in the garage?
6. Who do you think Doctor Death is? Why do you think he has this name?
7. What does the expression "see it with your mind's eye" mean?
8. Who does the sentence "He looked at me with a stupid grin on his face" refer to? What does it tell you about the attitude of the narrator?
9. What do the words "Mum and Dad took it all in" mean?
10. What do you think the baby was like? Why?

B. Read the excerpt from the second chapter of *Skellig* and answer the following questions.

Level 3

Chapter Two

1 I nearly got into the garage that Sunday morning. I took my own torch and shone it in. The outside doors to the back lane must have fallen off years ago and there were dozens of massive planks nailed across the entrance. The timbers holding the roof were rotten and the roof was sagging in. The bits of the floor you could see between the rubbish were full of cracks and holes. The people that took the rubbish out of the house were supposed to take it out of the garage as well, but they took one look at the place and said they wouldn't go in it even for danger money. There were old chests of drawers and broken washbasins and bags of cement, ancient doors leaning against the walls, deck chairs with the cloth seats rotted away. Great rolls of rope and cable hung from nails. Heaps of water pipes and great boxes of rusty nails were scattered on the floor. Everything was covered in dust and spiders' webs. There was mortar that had fallen from the walls. There was a little window in one of the walls but it was filthy and there were rolls of cracked **lino** standing in front of it. The place stank of rot and dust. Even the bricks

---

lino: (linoleum) floor covering, with a canvas backing

 ISBN-978-81-8477-734-5

were crumbling like they couldn't bear the weight anymore. It was like the whole thing was sick of itself and would collapse in a heap and have to get bulldozed away.

2 I heard something scratching in one of the corners, and something scuttling about, then it all stopped and it was just dead quiet in there.

3 I stood daring myself to go in.

4 I was just going to slip inside when I heard Mum shouting at me.

5 "Michael! What you doing?"

6 She was at the back door.

7 "Didn't we tell you to wait till we're sure it's safe?"

8 I stepped back and looked at her.

9 "Well, didn't we?" she shouted.

10 "Yes," I said.

11 "So keep out! All right?"

12 I shoved the door and it lurched half-shut on its single hinge.

13 "All right?" she yelled.

14 "All right," I said. "Yes. All right. All right."

15 "Do you not think we've got more to worry about than stupid you getting crushed in a stupid garage?"

16 "Yes."

17 "You just keep out, then! Right?"

18 "Right. Right, right, right."

19 Then I went back into the wilderness we called a garden and she went back to the flaming baby.

 ISBN-978-81-8477-734-5

11. What do the first few lines in Chapter One and Chapter Two tell you?
12. What does the expression "wouldn't go in it even for danger money" mean?
13. Why is the narrator interested in the garage?
14. What feelings does the narrator have towards his mother?
15. The following questions need you to think more deeply about the overall feelings expressed in both the chapters. Discuss them with a partner.
    - What is the narrator's attitude towards the baby?
    - What is the mother's mood like at first? How does it change and why?
    - How does she treat her son in Chapter Two? What is the reason behind her behaviour?
    - What is the narrator's general mood like?
    - Decide whether or not the garage could become important, and if so, why?
16. Write in separate paragraphs what you have inferred about the characters in *Skellig*.

Vocabulary

When the author describes the garage, he does so by giving plenty of detail so that a picture of the garage builds up in our minds. Sometimes, the author uses adjectives such as **filthy** and **pale,** but these are not overused.

A. Read the excerpt below and underline the words that give a new detail. Some examples are provided for you to start with. Use the same method for the remaining paragraph.

The outside doors to the back lane must have fallen off years ago and there were dozens of massive <u>planks nailed across the entrance</u>. The timbers holding the <u>roof</u> were <u>rotten</u> and the roof was <u>sagging in</u>.

 ISBN-978-81-8477-734-5

The bits of the floor you could see between the rubbish were full of cracks and holes. The people that took the rubbish out of the house were supposed to take it out of the garage as well, but they took one look at the place and said they wouldn't go in it even for danger money. There were old chests of drawers and broken washbasins and bags of cement, ancient doors leaning against the walls, deck chairs with the cloth seats rotted away. Great rolls of rope and cable hung from nails. Heaps of water pipes and great boxes of rusty nails were scattered on the floor. Everything was covered in dust and spiders' webs. There was mortar that had fallen from the walls. There was a little window in one of the walls but it was filthy and there were rolls of cracked lino standing in front of it. The place stank of rot and dust. Even the bricks were crumbling like they couldn't bear the weight anymore. It was like the whole thing was sick of itself and would collapse in a heap and have to get bulldozed away.

B. Do you know what purple prose is? It refers to a description that is showy and overdone. It may have overcomplicated words or repeat a description unnecessarily. Or it may have too many adjectives or adverbs. Read and compare A and B below.

A

It was a freezing, cold day and the glassy, white ice had gathered on the frosty window where it had woven clear, delicate patterns and where thin, spiky icicles hung from the frozen windowsill. It was truly cold and she could see her warm, hazy breath dancing about in front of her as it came out of her mouth.

B

It was so cold she could see her warm, hazy breath dancing around in front of her.

A is an example of purple prose, whereas **B** is a more effective description that conveys the same message.

 ISBN-978-81-8477-734-5

C. Write two short descriptions in purple prose from the suggestions listed below. Then give them to a partner to rewrite as suitable descriptions.

1. An eerie palace
2. Watching an eclipse of the sun
3. A storm at sea
4. A car chase
5. Eating an exotic dish for the first time
6. Riding a bicycle for the first time

Grammar

Writers often use various **tenses** in stories. This allows them to shift from past to present to future if they wish.

In the excerpts from *Skellig*, the events that are being narrated have happened in the past. However, more than one form of past tense has been used as shown in the example given below.

simple past tense

I **found** him in the garage on a Sunday afternoon. It was the day after we moved into Falconer Road. The winter was ending. Mum **had said** we'd be moving just in time for the spring.

past perfect tense – This tells us that what Mum said happened some time before "I found him..."

 ISBN-978-81-8477-734-5

A. Complete the following sentences. Each sentence should contain both the simple past tense and past perfect tense.

1. Yesterday, I gave the essay to my teacher...
2. My blue bike...
3. She understood the movie...
4. Although he...
5. Before I went to Goa,...
6. By the time...
7. At twelve noon...
8. With his bag over his shoulder...
9. On the other side of the road...
10. They felt bad about selling...

B. Fill in each blank with the correct form of the verb in brackets.

Example:
School finished yesterday and now we __________ in the garden. (play)
School finished yesterday and now we <u>are playing</u> in the garden.

1. As soon as Tim __________ homework, he rushed off to the tennis courts. (finish)
2. Lakshmi __________ on the new job from tomorrow. (start)
3. I __________ the vegetables yesterday so it should still be quite fresh. (buy)
4. Don't interrupt your sister while she __________. (study)
5. I __________, unless my parents don't object. (come)
6. Jenny __________ the play already, and she says it's very good. (see)
7. I was thinking about Jim, when all of a sudden he __________ into the room. (walk)

 ISBN-978-81-8477-734-5

8. There ______________ four of them. I had seen one of them before. (be)

9. Let me know as soon as Ravi ______________. (arrive)

10. If Shanti ______________, will she bring her sister with him? (come)

Listening

Listen to the text about David Almond and answer the following questions.

1. Where was David Almond born and when?
2. Name two other books apart from *Skellig* that David Almond has written. Can you remember the dates as well?
3. What important medal has the author won? Do you remember the name of the book for which he was awarded the medal?
4. What kind of ideas interest David Almond in his books?
5. What does the main character have to deal with?
6. What other forms of literature has Almond written?

Speaking

Write a commentary about what you think will happen in *Skellig* and present it to a group.

1. Refer back to the work you have done in the previous exercises and think of more than one possibility. Consider the following in particular.
    - what is happening in the family
    - the state of mind of the main character
    - the relationship between the main character and his mother
    - the garage as a focus of attention

 ISBN-978-81-8477-734-5

2. Present your ideas as a talk to a small group.
3. Listen to the comments of other group members.
4. Decide on the most likely outcome between you and partners in your group.

Writing

Describe an interesting setting and include one main character.

1. Choose one setting from the following:
    - A city street in the monsoon, with many colourful umbrellas
    - A tree house
    - A houseboat on the Jhelum river, Srinagar
    - Arriving on the moon
    - A wild backyard
    - At a beach
    - Playing football in the school ground

2. Ask yourself these questions before you begin.

- Is the setting ugly, beautiful, frightening, strange? Can you think of anything else?
- What is the most important aspect of the setting?
- What nouns are associated with the setting? Think of five and write them down.
- What is the mood of the setting? (For example, "tense", "leisurely" or "comical")
- What is your character doing?
- When is your story set in – in the present, past or future?

3. Give your description a title when you have finished writing it.

Activity

Work in groups of four to carry out a review of the work you did in the "Writing" task above.

1. You should read each other's work and make notes. Ask yourself the following questions.

- Can you see the description in your mind's eye?
- What part did you like the most?
- If you had to cut any section, which would it be?
- Which words do you think suited the description best?

 ISBN-978-81-8477-734-5

2. After completing the previous exercise, copy out the following and complete it with your notes. Make about six points, in total.

Description title:	
Strengths	**Weaknesses**

3. Discuss the notes for each piece of writing with the student who wrote it. When you consider what other people have written about your own work, you may find that opinions vary. You must decide what comments are most useful to you to improve your writing.

 ISBN-978-81-8477-734-5

Theme 6

Technology

A

B

Look at pictures A and B and answer the following questions.

1. Describe the difference between the two computers.
2. When do you think they date from?
3. How do you think computers in the future will differ?
4. How have computers affected your life?

 ISBN-978-81-8477-734-5

11 The World in Your Room

Dr Mike Goldsmith is a scientist and has written more than twenty non-fiction books for children. This excerpt is adapted from his book *Fantastic Future*.

1 If you're reading this in your bedroom, have a look round. If you're lucky, you'll see books and magazines. However, you will definitely find a mobile, a PC with email and Internet access, a TV, radio, various remote controls, maybe a few postcards and photos – in other words, your room is stuffed to bursting with various kinds of communication devices.

In what way is the layout of the text useful?

2 Over the last few centuries, a big chunk of the inventions people have come up with have been related in some way to communication, from posting letters to sending texts. Communication is something that people have always wanted to do. You were trying to do it as soon as you were born and well before you learned how (and it was very irritating for your parents). You'll probably spend the rest of your life talking, phoning, writing, emailing and texting thousands of people.

3 Our keenness to communicate means that, in a few years, your bedroom might look something like this:

Super-mobile phones

4 In your future bedroom, your mobile will beep for attention and then tell you that your favourite band is about to start their gig. You'll send

 ISBN-978-81-8477-734-5

a quick text to those of your friends who like that band (your mobile will know which friends these are), and you'll be able to see and hear their performance – also on your mobile, which will record the best bits for later, too.

What are the main areas covered in the text?

5 Today, almost everyone who can afford a mobile has got one. So, in order to continue selling them, the manufacturers have to keep coming up with new gizmos.

6 A few decades further in the future, and you won't have to fish your mobile out from the back of the sofa – it'll be constantly at your side (or more likely on your shoulder or perched on – or even in – your ear). By then, computer memory will be so economical that your mobile will record everything that happens to you – everything you see and hear – so that you'll be able to look back over what happened during the last day, or decade: whenever you like. Clever software will be included to gloss over the boring bits, not to mention those terribly embarrassing moments you'd rather draw a discreet veil over.

7 Mobiles like this will be very useful, and not just for you. They'll download their information to the Internet, where all sorts of people will be able to access it – so tracking down criminals, finding missing persons, and getting instant, readymade news bulletins will be easy. In fact, they'll be so useful that, chances are, mobiles will become compulsory one day.

Thought-controlled lights

8 This sounds very much out of a science fiction, but actually, the way they'll work isn't very complicated.

9 Imagine a whole world of thought-controlled gadgets that will work just like this. As well as inventions that respond to instructions that we deliberately "think" at them. There will be some gadgets that will sense our mood. Some of your bedroom furniture will even think! Like...

 ISBN-978-81-8477-734-5

Mind-reading bed cum chair

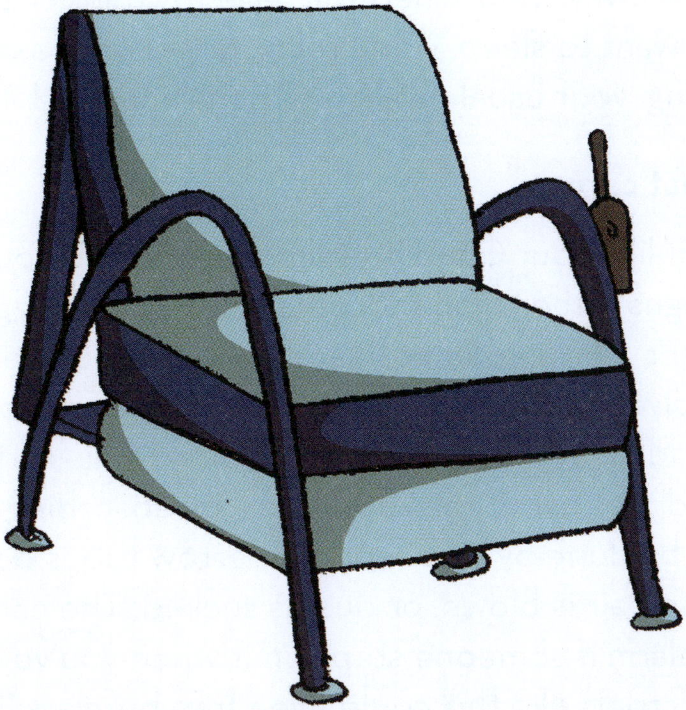

10 Your future bedroom might be a bit smaller than today's, with house prices rising and the population growing. So, instead of a bed, easy chair and office-type chair, you may have just one thing – maybe it'll be called Smart Chair, or perhaps a Ched or a Bair (actually, to be brutally honest, it might be called a Thunker for all I know – predicting what it's called is harder than predicting how it works). Anyway, imagine you've just finished your homework and it's time to listen to some music. Even as you think so, your "Ched" softens and reclines. Music comes out of it until you start to get sleepy, and the music softens and dies as the Ched gets wider, flatter and softer. It warms up a little, folds itself gently around and you fall peacefully asleep.

11 How does it work? Well, your brain produces regular patterns of electricity all the time, which depends on how you feel – these patterns change when you're alert, tired or asleep. Cheds will have built-in detectors that will pick up and recognise these patterns. When your Ched notices that you're sleepy, it will turn into a bed, and when you're ready for homework, it will be too. When you're ready to get up, the

 ISBN-978-81-8477-734-5

Ched will be able to straighten gradually into a column – and then fold itself neatly away. Your Ched will have to "think" – to decide whether you really want to sleep, work, relax, or get up, based on the time, what you're doing, your usual pattern of behaviour and all sorts of things.

Carpet that cares

12 This is a bit like your Ched. It will change to suit you, but it will react to physical signs rather than thoughts – it will be snuggly and warm on a cold winter's morning, smooth and cool on a June afternoon. This carpet will also solve that awful problem: do you let your parents into your room to clean it, do it yourself, or let it get dirty? This carpet will keep itself clean – and the rest of the room too – by absorbing dust from the air. All this could be done by a network of narrow tubes down through which cool or warm air is blown, or dust is sucked. The carpet will also act as a burglar alarm if someone steps on it when you've told it you're out. Perhaps, carpets like this could even trap burglars like flies in a web, by squirting a network of sticky threads over them that harden in the air.

Virtual Reality system

13 Virtual Reality (VR) involves a computer producing sounds, images and physical sensations so realistic that they can convince us that they're real. It's not as easy as it seems because what we sense depends on how we move. Also, even the best VR systems around today don't **generate** smell or taste, and physical sensations are limited to a few **prods** and presses on the inside surface of a glove you wear, or some jerks and wobbles of your chair. The easiest bit of a VR system to get to work is the audio system – stereo headphones are all you need. Stereo headphones were around even before your parents were of your age, practically forever, in other words. Getting a realistic picture isn't too difficult either – for a three-dimensional effect, all you need are two tiny screens that show slightly different views, one for each eye. Of course,

---

generate: make, create
prod: poke, jab, nudge

 ISBN-978-81-8477-734-5

when thought technology takes off, all these equipments will seem as outdated as a suit of armour. Just a little chip attached to your head - or surgically implanted into it - might do all the feeding of signals directly to the parts of your brain you use for seeing, hearing, touching, tasting and smelling.

Rewritable books

14 In your futuristic bedroom, you might have only one book. At the press of a button - or a spoken word from you - its pages will change from a comic to a history book (when it's time to do your homework), and then maybe to a TV guide, A to Z, or the latest title, depending on what sort of evening you have in mind. Rewritable books like this will look like ordinary books, but with thicker, glossier pages. Each page will have thousands of tiny spheres **embedded** in it. The spheres will be white on top and black underneath. When the book receives a computer file of data, some spheres will turn over, making black dots appear in groups, forming letters and pictures.

---

embedded: fixed, implanted

 ISBN-978-81-8477-734-5

Reading Comprehension

Answer the following questions based on your understanding of the passage.

Level 1

1. What electronic devices would one find in one's room these days?
2. What do many of the new inventions of the last decade have in common?
3. In future, how might you be informed that your favourite band is about to play?
4. Where might you keep your mobile phones in future?
5. What would rooms in the future be like?
6. What is the main advantage of a Smart Chair?
7. What does VR stand for and what does it mean?

Level 2

8. What would be the advantages of a smart mobile phone?
9. What would be the main disadvantage if a mobile recorded everything that happened to you?
10. Write a note on a comic situation about a chair that can think!
11. Write three sentences describing the "carpet that cares".

Level 3

12. A chip implant of the future could enhance the experience of VR. Describe in your own words what this might feel like.
13. Of all the gadgets mentioned, which appeals to you most? Give reasons to support your choice.

 ISBN-978-81-8477-734-5

Vocabulary

Many new words are created when new inventions are made. In English, these new words are often drawn from Ancient Greek and Latin (the language of the Romans). Consider the word "technology", and see how it has evolved as explained below.

technology — *techne* (Greek) meaning skill, art
— *lego* (Greek) meaning "I speak"

Some more words are elaborated here for your convenience.

engine — *in* (Latin) meaning "in"
— *gignere* (Latin) meaning "create"

locomotive — *loco* (Latin) meaning "place"
— *motivus* (Latin) meaning "motive"

A. Find the origins of these words from the text and write them down.

Word	Origin
photograph	
telephone	
mobile	
gizmo	
computer	
audio	
stereophonic	
chatbot	

 ISBN-978-81-8477-734-5

Word	Origin
camera	
cannon	
tram	
truck	

B. Work in pairs and discuss how the meaning of the above words link to their origins.

C. Discuss why the Smart Chair might be called a Ched or a Bair.

D. Fill in the blanks with the words related to various aspects of technology listed in the box.

dwarf	nanotechnology	predecessor	naked
progress	gigabytes	microbes	miniaturisation
terabytes	technology	hardware	vessels

We often think that ______________ is shown as things get bigger and bigger. Buildings get taller, bridges get longer, roads get wider – more and more people have more and more things. The memory of household computers used to be measured in kilobytes. It is now usually measured in ______________ or even ______________ – a unit that is almost a billion times the size of the kilobyte.

But thinking about computers should remind us that size is not everything. Though the memory of a modern household computer may ______________ that of a model built 20 years ago, the contemporary machine

 ISBN-978-81-8477-734-5

itself is probably much smaller and neater than its ____________. We might also say that, as ____________ advances, it gets smaller. We have already seen the benefits of ____________ not only in computer ____________ but also in cameras that are small enough to be inserted into the human body and travel through organs and blood ____________. ____________ promises to create machines that are even smaller, no bigger than tiny ____________ – though, for most of us, it is difficult to imagine how you can construct things that are too small to be seen by the ____________ eye.

Grammar

A **conditional clause** is a subordinate clause that says what the circumstances are for something to happen.

conditional clause (the laptop will work on condition that it has a new battery)

The laptop won't work **unless you buy a new battery**.

Conditional clauses may begin with words such as "if", "unless", "as long as", "providing", "only if", "on condition". A few more examples are given below:

If water boils, it turns to steam.

When he eats breakfast, he feels better all day.

A. Complete these sentences with a conditional clause or a main clause. Make sure all the examples above are used.

1. ... if state-of-the-art technology is created.
2. You can use the mobile...
3. ... as long as you have all the necessary components.
4. At present, they can't do anything...

 ISBN-978-81-8477-734-5

5. He would be happy to lend you his gizmo...
6. ... only if you can click the right buttons!
7. ... he'll pass the exams.
8. She won't come back ...
9. ... I get up at seven.
10. ... we will have to start the meeting without him.

B. Complete the following sentences either with the conjunction "if" or the conjunction "unless".

1. ______________ my calculations are correct, they owe us $2,000.
2. You won't get to the airport on time ______________ you hurry up.
3. She is absolutely certain to fail ______________ she works harder.
4. ______________ it had not been for Ravi's prompt action, many more lives might have been lost.
5. ______________ anyone can think of a better one, I suggest we stick to our original plan.
6. We'll go in Samira's car – ______________ that's OK with you, Samira.
7. ______________ the bullet had gone in 2 millimetres higher, he would undoubtedly have been killed.
8. ______________ I'm very much mistaken, that's Linda Lee, the film star, over there.

Listening

Listen carefully to the text about virtual friends and answer the questions.

1. What is a virtual friend called?
2. What features does the imaginary friend mentioned in the text have? Try to remember all of the six features.

 ISBN-978-81-8477-734-5

Speaking

Design your own futuristic gadget.

1. To help you make a decision, think on the following lines.
   - Will your gadget be for children, adults, pets - who?
   - Will it be used indoors, outdoors or both?
   - Will it be carried around or fixed?
   - Will your gadget be comic or have a serious purpose? (Try not to make your gadget too complicated.)
2. Create a diagram of your gadget and label it clearly.
3. Then, present your gadget to a small group explaining how it works.

Writing

Refer to the gadget you designed under "Speaking" and create a witty advertisement for it.

1. Remember who your target audience is and try to include all or some of the following.
   - Clear images of your product showing how it works
   - Persuasive language *(It's smart, it's stylish, it's perfect.)*
   - A jingle, short sentences or catchy slogans that use the imperative (*Buy one, get one free!)*
   - Words that address the reader directly *(It's smart, it's stylish, it's perfect. It's you!)*

 ISBN-978-81-8477-734-5

2. Think about how it will be advertised. Would you sell it locally or nationally? Would you advertise through a website, a digital billboard, a poster, a newspaper or a leaflet? This will affect how you present your advertisement.

3. Remember, an advertisement can present a product in a good light, but it should not claim the product can do things that it cannot do.

Activity

Carry out some research to find out how people lived before the advent of modern technology. This would be approximately 150 or 200 years ago.

1. Remember, this is a time when we didn't have any of the following gizmos.

   - computers
   - mobile phones or telephones
   - televisions
   - radios
   - cars
   - gas supply
   - washing machines
   - fridges and freezers
   - vacuum cleaners and other domestic products
   - electricity
   - cookers

 ISBN-978-81-8477-734-5

2. In particular, find out how people cooked, heated, lighted and cleaned their homes, preserved foods and travelled.

3. Make notes and use them to create a fact file and a written account of what you have found out.

 ISBN-978-81-8477-734-5

12 What Games Do You Play?

Though summarising and paraphrasing a text are similar, there is also an important difference.

1. When we summarise, we condense the text, using our own words. In other words, we sum up what the text means.
2. When we paraphrase, we use our own words but keep the original information. We do not sum it up.

Skimming and scanning a text can help you summarise and paraphrase.

A. Refer to the passage below and complete the following exercises.

1. Skim each paragraph to gain an overall impression of its meaning.
2. Scan for keywords, phrases or sentences that tell you the main point or points of the paragraph. This has been done for your reference in the first paragraph.

B. Make notes when you scan.

Now read the following extract.

1 Is it basketball, table tennis, football or chess? It may well be video games. If it is, you may need to think about just how much time you spend playing. Are you overly preoccupied with games? Are you fixed to the screen whenever you have a spare minute or do you have other hobbies too? These are important considerations. **Video games are often young people's main choice of entertainment and they can have their downside.**

 ISBN-978-81-8477-734-5

2 Why? The simple reason is that playing video games too often and for too long is not good for your health, and this means health in the broadest context. That is to say, it isn't good for you physically, nor is it good for you mentally. It can affect concentration and young people who are obsessed with interactive games can become irritable and angry, even violent. We assume this is because the kinds of stories told in video games can often depict violence of some kind. For a long time, violent depictions in video games have been a major concern for parents and teachers. This does not mean that most young people are affected. However, the evidence shows that with exposure to violent video games, some young people can become more hostile, particularly if they lose their temper easily and don't get along with others anyway. *(Science Daily, June 2010)*

3 Playing video games for longer duration also affects one's physical health. Constant repetition can cause "gamer's thumb", which is a swelling caused by too much use of the gamepad. It doesn't take much to see that if you're constantly sitting in front of a monitor, you're not being active enough. Being physically active should get the blood circulating round the body. It also makes you feel good, and if you play team sports, you are interacting with others.

 ISBN-978-81-8477-734-5

4 There is another problem with video games. They don't encourage you to be with others. We need to be solitary sometimes, but we also need company. Humans are social animals and we develop our social skills by having friends and being with our family. In addition, young people who are constantly playing video games can also neglect their homework and be less involved in their schoolwork.

5 So, amidst all this doom and gloom, do video games have any benefits? They probably do. They can encourage good motor skills, such as helping your hands and eyes to work well together. They can also encourage thinking skills. After all, you have to solve problems when you are playing a game and that's also what you have to do in school. The feeling of success you feel when you win a game can also spur you on to success in other areas, and some educational games may improve performance in mathematics. And while video games may not be very good for enhancing concentration, they may be beneficial when it comes to tasks that require shifting attention quickly.

6 Like most things in life, the key to reap only benefits from video games is the word "moderation". You should try to balance your game-playing with other aspects of life, such as spending time with your family and friends and taking up hobbies that allow you to get fresh air and physical exercise.

 ISBN-978-81-8477-734-5

Reading Comprehension

Answer the following questions.

1. In order to sum up or paraphrase a text in your own words, you will need to use synonyms, which are words that have the same or similar meaning. Find the synonyms for the following words. (Use a thesaurus if you need to.) They all come from the passage *What Games Do You Play?*

   - preoccupied
   - context
   - concentration
   - exposure
   - solitary
   - encourage
   - moderation
   - spare
   - evidence
   - depictions
   - interacting
   - neglect
   - enhancing
   - spending

2. Using the work you have done so far, in not more than 150 words, sum up the passage *What Games Do You Play?*

Remember

When you summarise a text, you sum up what it means.

3. Some words and sentences in the passage **add to**, **develop** or **contrast with** the main points. Write down notes to these questions.

   - Beside video games, what activities are mentioned?
   - Which two questions in the first paragraph ask the same thing in different ways?
   - Two examples of the effects of video games are discussed. What are they?
   - In the passage, what are the benefits of being physically active?

 ISBN-978-81-8477-734-5

- What points are made about being human?
- What benefits of video games are mentioned?
- What other things should you do apart from playing video games?

4. Now using the work you have done, paraphrase the text in your own words. You do not have to mention every detail, but you must include the main points and explain these points further where you think it is important.

Remember

When you paraphrase, you write the same thing using different words.

 ISBN-978-81-8477-734-5

Vocabulary

Antonym means opposite. So, an antonym is the opposite meaning of a word.

Word	Antonym
long	short
solitary	social
expose	guard
success	failure

A. Write down the antonyms for the words below. They all come from the passage *What Games Do You Play?*

1. important
2. active
3. encourage
4. reason
5. involved
6. attention
7. evidence
8. concentration
9. moderation
10. violent
11. angry
12. spare

B. Now think of antonyms for these words without looking in a thesaurus.

1. fixed
2. simple
3. often
4. broadest
5. major
6. physical
7. ugly
8. mellow
9. intelligent
10. courage

 ISBN-978-81-8477-734-5

C. Change each word in the list into a word of the opposite meaning by adding a prefix.

1. action
2. civilised
3. employment
4. freeze
5. mobility
6. noble
7. pleasure
8. regularity
9. responsibility
10. service

 ISBN-978-81-8477-734-5

Grammar

Modal verbs allow us to express many different feelings or ideas as shown in the example below.

"should" expresses likelihood – It is likely that the cream will help relieve the pain.

This soothing cream **should** help to relieve the pain.

"should" expresses advice – Perhaps it is best to cook the vegetables for less time.

Perhaps you **should** think about cooking the vegetables in less time.

The common modal verbs are – should, would, could, can, will, may, might, must, shall. Some more examples of usage of modal verbs are given below:

They **can** control their own budgets.

Could I borrow your dictionary?

China **may** become a major economic power.

They **might** give us a discount.

A. Underline the modal verb in each sentence below.

1. You could give your old video games to your cousin.
2. I shall definitely buy Ali a video game for his birthday, and I know which one he would like.
3. You can play your new video game if you've finished all your homework.
4. Being physically active should get the blood circulating round the body.
5. You should try to balance your game-playing with other hobbies.
6. The feeling of success you have when you win a game can also spur you on to succeed in other areas.
7. Shall I help you with your luggage?

 ISBN-978-81-8477-734-5

8. Profits should increase next year.
9. It will happen if you work hard for it.
10. We must leave for station now if we want to catch the train.

B. Decide how it is being used and then complete the table. Refer to the box below for the possible uses of the modal verbs.

permission	certainty	likelihood	advice / suggestion
possibility	obligation	preference	prediction

Modal verb	Use
a)	
b)	
c)	
d)	
e)	
f)	
g)	
h)	
i)	
j)	

 ISBN-978-81-8477-734-5

C. Fill in each blank with the most suitable modal verb given in the brackets.

1. Sarah thinks that she ______________ be able to come, but she's not sure. (may / could / must)
2. If this house ______________ speak, it would have some fascinating stories to tell. (should / might / could)
3. I ______________ rely on Mary to help, if I were you. She's extremely busy at the moment. (mustn't / wouldn't / won't)
4. You really ______________ clean these windows, they're terribly dirty. (ought to / can / would)
5. You ______________ bring any food, we've got plenty here. (mightn't / mustn't / needn't)
6. They ______________ have left some cake for us, instead of eating it all themselves. (must / might / will)
7. They aren't answering the door, so they ______________ have left already. (should / need to / must)

D. Modal verbs can also be used in the negative. Write a dialogue between a brother and sister who are quarrelling, using the following.

couldn't	shan't	won't	can't	shouldn't	mightn't

Set the dialogue out correctly. For example:

Padma: You shouldn't be staying up so late.

Pratap: Why can't I stay up late.

 ISBN-978-81-8477-734-5

Listening

Listen to the comments on video games carefully.

1. As you do so, make a note of the main point in each one.
2. Decide whether or not these people are "for" or "against" video games.
3. Complete the table.

Who?	Main point	For or against?
Teenage boy		
Father		
Teenage girl		
Teacher (female)		
Mother		
Teacher (male)		

 ISBN-978-81-8477-734-5

Speaking

A. Work in pairs. Discuss the points made under "Listening".

B. Think of two more points of your own that are in favour of and against video games. Make notes.

For	Against
1.	1.
2.	2.
3.	3.

Speaking Tips

- Try to be coherent and explain your ideas clearly.
- Listen to other comments carefully.
- Be prepared to change your mind.

Writing

Now write an account on video games, saying whether or not you think they are valuable.

1. Remember you have to choose a "for" or "against" position.
2. Add other viewpoints that were previously discussed.
3. Write using your own words.

 ISBN-978-81-8477-734-5

4. Write clearly and interestingly.

5. Use connectors to help you present your point of view.

Activity

Create a leaflet, as a series of recommendations, about watching video games.

1. Draw on the work you have done and think about the following points.
   - Video games that are useful
   - Video games that you should avoid
   - The length of viewing time
   - How old you should be before you play video games
2. Make your leaflet user-friendly (for example, use bullet points).
3. Include illustrations.

 ISBN-978-81-8477-734-5